THE POLICE
L'Historia Bandido
By Phil Sutcliffe and Hugh Fielder

PROTEUS BOOKS
London and New York

PROTEUS BOOKS is an imprint of
The Protus Publishing Group

United States
PROTEUS PUBLISHING CO., INC.
733 Third Avenue
New York, N.Y. 10017
distributed by:
THE SCRIBNER BOOK COMPANIES, INC.
597, Fifth Avenue
New York, N.Y. 10017

United Kingdom
PROTEUS (PUBLISHING) LIMITED
Bremar House,
Sale Place,
London, W2 1PT.

ISBN 0 906071 66 6 (p/b)
ISBN 0 906071 77 1 (h/b)

First published in US 1981
First published in UK 1981

© 1981 Hugh Fielder and Phil Sutcliffe,
The Proteus Publishing Group
All rights reserved.

Printed and bound in Italy by
New Interlitho

Other titles in the **PROTEUS ROCKS** series:
**THE BEATLES APART
THE DAVID BOWIE PROFILE
KATE BUSH
ELVIS COSTELLO
LED ZEPPELIN 1969-1980
NEW WAVE EXPLOSION
QUEEN
ROCK BOTTOM: THE BEST OF THE WORST OF ROCK
VISIONS OF ROCK
WHATEVER HAPPENED TO . . ?**

CONTENTS

INTRO: AT THE RITZ

Chapter 1 **STEWART: THE RIGHT PLACE AT THE RIGHT TIME (EVENTUALLY)**
Chapter 2 **STING: TRY PLAYING SCRABBLE WITH HIM**
Chapter 3 **WE'RE GONNA PLAY SOME PUNK NOW**
Chapter 4 **ANDY: HAVE YOU MET MY GUITARIST?**
Chapter 5 **THERE'S JUST ONE THING, YOU HAVE TO BE BLOND**
Chapter 6 **BLOOD AND GUTS AND GROTTY MOTELS**
Chapter 7 **WORLD TOUR: EVEN THE SHEEP RIOTED**
Chapter 8 **WALKING ROUND THE ROOM**
Chapter 9 **OUTRO: HERE'S SHIRLEY, SHE'S A BIG FAN OF THE BAND**

L'Historia Bandido wouldn't have been possible without the cooperation of Stewart Copeland, Sting and Andy Summers. They and everyone else we spoke to told us more than we asked.

Thanks to...
The Police family: Stewart Copeland and Sonja Kristina, Andy and Kate Summers, Sting and Frances Tomelty, Miles Copeland and Mary Pegg, Ian and Connie Copeland, Kim and Kate Turner.

Back-up vocals: Henry Padovani, Nigel Gray, Nick Jones, Vermillion Sands, Al Clark, Zoot Money, Gerry Richardson, Andy Hudson, Dave Wood, Derek and Kat Burbidge.

Cutting us down to size: Dave Hepworth.

Others without whom: Anna and Chloe Fielder, Gay Lee, Keith Altham, Anne Freeman, Larry Burnett, Dave Fudger, Jill Furmanovsky, Martin Bailey, Kelly Pike, Pippa Markham, Claudine, Brian Munns, Doreen Boyd, Trevor Byfield, Nick Locke, Fenella Greenfield, Pete Frame, Alan 'Nelson' Lewis.

Background sources (and about three stolen quotes): Sounds, NME (article by Paul Morley), Musicians Only, Look Now, Music Week, Shields Weekly News, Patches, Record Mirror, Sunday Times (Gordon Burn), Rolling Stone, Daily Mirror, Smash Hits, Trouser Press, Melody Maker (Allan Jones) and 'The Real Spy World' by Miles Copeland.

Editor Nicola Hodge

Book design by Zena Flax

INTRO: AT THE RITZ

On Monday, January 12, 1981, Sting sat on the chintzy sofa in his 400-dollar-a-night New York hotel suite probing a mountainous strawberry confection the room service waiter had just brought him and said "I'm so frustrated".

Two nights earlier the Police had played their successful debut at Madison Square Garden, the biggest concert of their career. Then the next night they had gone to the little Ritz Theater, a 'street credibility' gig and as far as Sting was concerned he'd blown it. He was depressed and that opened him up to all kinds of gloomy ruminations about the state he and the Police were in: "I wasn't doing very well last night was I? I didn't want to pretend I was enjoying myself. And the more the audience didn't seem to notice that, the more annoyed I got. Very selfish. A shameful performance by me.

"It's fatigue. We're pushing this as far as it will go. It's really starting to tell on me. I'm a bit worried at this juncture.

"Last night I felt as if I'd done the songs too many times. I'd never had that feeling before. I was really bad, just ... inconsolable. I'd forgotten what I was singing about. It was a terrible anticlimax after the Garden as well.

"I used to be a glorious amateur and love every minute. My whole week was centered on waiting for Wednesday night when my old band Last Exit played the Gosforth Hotel in Newcastle. But now it's such a pain to get through a show — actual physical pain in my throat I mean. You can hear it."

Very few bands carry on growing artistically after they've 'made it'.

Stewart Copeland knows it: "It's almost impossible for us to blow people's minds any more. We don't freak people out. At a gig it looks as though it's all happening, but these days it's prescribed, it's premeditated, it's been generated by our records and everything we've done before. We need to turn on new people, to change new minds, start new hysteria and there's nowhere left to go."

Rock stardom is a roller-coaster — a wonderful ride if you have a strong stomach. The Police undoubtedly have. But, as Stewart insists, they are not Abba or a cabaret group whose *sole* reason for being is the pursuit of success. They are often adventurous, innovative, exciting. As a genuine rock band their urge to make music is in the soul and bloodstream: the paradox is that the reward, vast wealth, is potentially harmful.

You're a megastar. You can buy the Empire State Building. You can't walk down the street alone (or imagine you can't, an even more dangerous condition). Stars lose touch with their fans. They lose touch with themselves. It's impossible to say which comes first. They forget what they're singing about. They forget why they're doing it. Some of them have a good time. Some of them die. Few survive intact.

Perhaps only the chameleons like David Bowie or Bob Dylan who have the gift of re-creating themselves time and again in different guises can manage it in the long term. They sustain inspiration on a level which transcends money because it ignores it.

By 1981 the Police had reached the top. For three years they'd moved too fast for the rot to set in. Then they decided to stop and take a look at themselves.

1
STEWART: THE RIGHT PLACE AT THE RIGHT TIME (EVENTUALLY)

"You can put it like this. Losing my virginity coincided with the first night I ever played in a group. I was led off down the beach by a girl three years older than me and I was shown the way so to speak. Which is significant I suppose: the first time I get my rocks off is the night I join a band." Stewart Copeland was maybe 14.

"But I was such a wimpy little kid I'm surprised even that was enough to do it for me. I'm proud of it though!"

Well that was one thing about growing up in Beirut.

Stewart Armstrong Copeland was born on July 16, 1952, in Alexandria, Virginia, on the outskirts of Washington, D.C. He was the youngest of four children: Miles Axe Copeland the Third, now manager of the Police, was born in London in 1944; Leonora (Lennie) in America in 1946; Ian, now the Police's agent in America, in Damascus, Syria, in 1949.

The reason for this exotic scattering of birthplaces was their father, Miles Axe Copeland the Second, a most unusual man, a hero to his sons and a profound influence on them.

Miles 2's own father was a liberal, community-minded doctor in Birmingham, Alabama, but whatever pressures there were on Miles 2 as a young man to follow in father's footsteps he evidently wasn't having any of it – he went out on the road as a jazz musician. In the 30s of course this was just as much a rebellion for a middle-class kid as joining a rock band is today. His sons assert that he was "one of the best jazz trumpeters of his era" and there's no need to doubt that when you consider that he played alongside Glen Miller, later one of the great swing band leaders.

So that's the music in the bloodline. But the Second World War put a stop to Miles 2's erstwhile freewheeling career: he joined the army and found himself in the intelligence wing, the OSS, and transferred to Eisenhower's staff in London, planning secret operations in Europe. He had discovered his niche and never played trumpet professionally again – though his children certainly inherited a talent for blowing their own.

The English posting also led Miles 2 to his wife, Lorraine, an eminent archaeologist, daughter of a doctor and a Scottish Opera singer. Miles 3 was born in the London of the flying-bomb and V2 rocket blitz. Then with the war in Europe won, Miles 2 went home to sort out how the talents he had developed might become a 'career' in peacetime. The answer was the Central Intelligence Agency.

He played a part in setting up the structure of the CIA, before being sent out as a field officer himself, initially in Damascus. He cut his teeth by overthrowing the Syrian government. The story is the family's favorite legend.

As 'an ordinary embassy political attaché' he was entertaining some senior Syrian army officers to dine and wine at his home when conversation turned to the current régime and, as Stewart tells it, "They thought the guy running Syria was an asshole and they could do better". Someone said in effect "How about it then?" and, says Stewart, "My father thought 'Let's give it a go'."

What the conspirators needed was an outbreak of public disorder to prove that the government had lost control and that the military should take a hand to restore order. Miles 2 came up with the ideal solution: why didn't they have a bunch of anonymous roughnecks drop round and shoot up his house, American Embassy property, thereby creating a diplomatic incident and clearly establishing his own innocence at the same time? Done? They fixed the day and time.

As a considerate father and husband Miles 2 naturally arranged for five-year-old Miles 3 and his very pregnant wife to be staying with friends in the mountains that night – in fact Lorraine gave birth to Ian while she was there. Probably he gave the servants the night off too, then sat and waited. Waited a long time.

Stewart portrays him getting on the phone to the conspirators: "Look, I thought we said nine o'clock. It's nearly midnight and those guys haven't showed. Can't you move 'em along? I want to get to bed." When the bars closed and the rentamob wandered over at last, he was back on the phone again, though perhaps from under the table this time: "Hey! You forgot to tell them to use blanks! They're making a terrible mess of the furniture. Damn, I'll have to hang up now – they're shooting at me personally."

The bullet-ridden Persian carpet holds a place of honor at the Copeland home in St. John's Wood, London, to this day and testifies to the short-term success of Miles 2's venture. The president was indeed overthrown, but five months later the usurpers were themselves deposed by another bunch of discontented army officers.

Miles 3 sees the incident as his father's and the CIA's 'cowboy days'. His own memory of that night is that "I resented being put out of our house so much! I hated poached eggs from that day on because that's what they gave us to eat up in the mountains."

The family cooled out in the States for a couple of years after that and Stewart was born in Virginia. Then, when he was nine months old, his father was posted to Cairo, Egypt, to help the new régime of Gamal Nasser set up a secret police force. The burly Egyptian president was a regular guest for dinner at the Copeland house and in fact his bodyguard, Hassan Duhamey, lived next door. Young Miles used to pop over and play with his machine-guns — and nearly 30 years later was to call on him for a more significant favor.

Egypt is an archaeologist's paradise as well as a volatile modern state and Lorraine Copeland was in her element there. Ian recalls that when he was a toddler every Sunday the family would go to a different pyramid or ancient temple for a picnic: "Our photograph albums are full of us standing in front of some enormous ruin in the middle of the desert."

When that assignment was completed Miles 2 and family hopped back to America again before settling in Beirut, Lebanon, for ten years from 1957, Stewart's formative years. It seems that it was about this time that the patriarch Copeland ceased being a full-time CIA employee though he was still in touch with the Agency on a freelance and advisory basis until the early 70s at least (as he reports openly in his books *The Game of Nations* and *The Real Spy World*). Miles 3 describes his father's subsequent line of work thus: "He went on to form his own sort of private CIA representing companies such as Pan-American airlines and Mobil oil in the Middle East because he could cut through all the garbage and go straight to the dictator who was running the country." Ian says: "We lived in Beirut mainly because it was a safe base for the family so dad could go off and do his dirty work" (this with a smile — he admires his father as fiercely as either of his brothers). Well, it did provide some interesting archaeological sites for their mother too. She later wrote a book about her study of Lebanese flints!

Miles 2's influence on his brood can hardly be overstated. He was and is a maverick constantly willing to disobey his 'superiors' and he has a frontiersman's sense of 'democracy'. That is, he believes in freedom to such an extent that the will of the majority is to be discounted unless it accords with his own opinions and wishes. The motto he quotes at the end of *The Real Spy World* is: "Somebody has to protect the strong from the weak". Such cavalier and cheerful rugged individualism is at the heart of the Copeland spirit as expressed more recently in the extraordinary career of the Police.

Stewart says he didn't know anything about his father's clandestine activities until his first book was published in 1969. He breathed the atmosphere though. If Beirut was a 'safe' place to grow up in, as Ian suggests, the Bronx is a nunnery and Soho a Buddhist retreat.

Beirut is the capital of the Lebanon, a Mediterranean port whose population has rapidly grown to nearly a million and flung crowds of people of different religion and culture together too fast for assimilation. The conflicts between them are perpetually erupting in skirmishes and sometimes civil war.

The Copeland brothers lived in luxury with half a dozen servants at their beck and call. It couldn't be said though that this was amid the suffering and starvation that, for example, the Police were to encounter much later in Bombay. Beirut is very westernized in some ways: nearly all its citizens own TVs and they are fanatical cinemagoers too. Real culture!

Essentially you couldn't live a sheltered existence in Beirut no matter who your parents were. Stewart's first solid recollections are of the civil war in 1958 when there was a general strike, kidnappings and street violence of every sort: "I was just a toddler, but I remember explosions in the night, sandbags and tanks in the street, gangs fighting and gunfire at any time. We were living in an apartment with the rooms full of food and the bathtubs full of water. Then the American fleet arrived on the horizon and the war was over. The American tanks unloaded and drove through the silent, empty streets and everything was peaceful ... until it broke up again later."

So he had plenty of excitement that didn't come the way of kids of his age growing up in the US or the UK — such as Sting. However looking back he reckons it was a "third-rate childhood" when it came to more homely pleasures. He had to watch *The Virginian* dubbed into Arabic — even though he and his brothers all spoke the language fluently it didn't sound right somehow.

Unlike Ian, he couldn't escape from his obvious status as a foreigner and outsider. He attended the American school for a while, then the English, without distinguishing himself. "All I knew was I was white and different and this wasn't my country anyway. I was a late developer in every respect. I was physically small for my age, bespectacled, utterly dreadful at my lessons, a real population statistic."

In terms of music he was too young for Elvis and the original rock 'n' roll explosion of course, and all he'd heard before the Beatles was the Top Twenty on BBC World Service or Voice of America radio wafting out of Miles 3's room — except when their father had been back to England or America and bought all the hit singles for them. The earliest favorite Stewart can recall was the Shadows, Cliff Richard's backing band who had a string of instrumental hits in the early 60s.

In January, 1963, when the Beatles' 'Please Please Me' was breaking through, Stewart was far more interested in the world-shaking events taking place on his doorstep. Harold 'Kim' Philby, a close friend of his father's was suddenly exposed as having been a Russian master spy.

The first even Miles 2 knew of it was when Philby vanished. But it affected his whole family. Philby's kids were friendly with his. Young Miles used to give them judo lessons and little Stewart would earn some pocket money and the odd trip to the movies by being thrown around as the 'dummy'. "Imagine what they had to live with," Stewart reflects. "First of all daddy disappears. That's a bit traumatic. Then there's all sorts of talk about Russians and spies and suddenly it turns out that daddy *is* a Russian spy!"

Still, in the best traditions of the gentlemen's club of

"I saw Curved Air the other night and I could not believe the dynamic force of their percussionist." Letter to a British music paper, 1975.

Stewart Copeland with Curved Air: "I felt I was going to be fired at any moment."

Intelligence, Miles senior rallied round Philby's family, helping them to sell up their furniture when they left Beirut.

The Lebanon was exciting, but the Copeland family was an experience in itself. Little Stewart had stupendous siblings.

He's sure that his father deliberately trained Miles 3 to be, in effect, a chip off the old block both mentally and physically: "He still has all the books my father gave him. *How To Shake The Money Tree, How To Win Friends And Influence People, Get On Top In Your Job, How To Make The Best Of Your Personality*. Courses in public speaking, everything you could imagine. He was preparing Miles to be an oil man amongst the Arabs actually."

Indeed Miles 3 was his father's son above everything. Not much of it was imposed on him; he wanted it. Talking about his father he's lyrical and inspired as a preacher: "Nobody else has a father as unique as ours! He's a total genius! A maverick! He has a great sense of humor! He's a very interesting person."

During his teens these influences brought out the fanatic streak in Miles. Between the ages of 16 and 18 he renounced smoking and alcohol, became a vegetarian and meditated or did yoga for five hours a day — this was years before the hippy era made such things fashionable: "I even used to wake up every morning at the same moment and go to the bathroom at the same moment. It was a total ascetic regimen until I started going to college in the States where it was impossible to keep it up."

At that stage the only way he had been a disappointment to his father was in his failure with the trumpet. Of course, Miles senior had bought him one when he was a youngster, but he had inherited none of his father's talent and the instrument didn't mean a thing to him anyway. Guitar ruled the rock 'n' roll he was into. "I do wish to hell he hadn't tried to foist that trumpet on me," he laments. "It's a family joke." He never liked letting his father down though.

So Miles 3 was a simmering, intense, energetic presence in the household obviously trying to emulate his father and often, in his absence, trying to stand in for him in the family heirarchy. The natural reaction of the younger children was rebellion against them both.

Lennie wouldn't have any truck with her father's presumption that she would be 'an elegant young lady' and subsequently a diplomat's wife. She studied furiously, one way and another bemusing Miles and amusing Ian. The Copeland family electricity crackles through their reminiscences of her.

Miles: "She's more dedicated than the rest of us put together. A *heavy* achiever. Very intense. In her early days she was very difficult."

Ian: "The thing was Miles would beat up on Lennie so she figured she had to side with me."

Miles: "I didn't beat her up!"

Ian: "You did!"

Miles: "She used to do things that infuriated me..."

Ian: "So you would drag her down the stairs!"

Miles: "She would do this (*holds a hand a few inches in front of his face*) and go 'I'm not touching you, I'm not touching you' and after two or three hours of that, OK, *whop!* 'It's my space too you know!'"

Ian: "She also used to dissect cats and things."

Miles: "Yeah, the famous Lennie story is she had a pet rabbit called Harvey and one day we came home and didn't see him and asked where he was and she produced these bottles. Here was the eyes and here was the ... eeeuch! That was our sister? This ghoulish being?"

Still there doesn't seem much doubt that Lennie wanted out of such a male-orientated household. Head down, she got 'straight As' in everything. In her late teens she attended the prestigious Vassar college in the States and went on to carve out an entirely independent career in the Californian film industry. Miles now harbors a notion that he might at last be able to tie her into the family enterprise through the Police's movie explorations.

Now Ian ... well, he made the others pale by comparison. The complete black sheep at 14. As Miles has it "He went A-rab". Or nearly. His playmates were Beirut's hellraising motorcycle gangs and his best friend was The King Of Death. Ian was known as Jodang or 'Little Rat'. Significantly, if Miles looked up the family tree and saw his father, little Stewart looked up and saw Ian: his hero, "He was like the Fonz you know".

About '63 or '64 the black-and-white clash between Ian and Miles came to a head when the elder brother got back from a year of his History and Political Science course at Birmingham Southern University, Alabama, and their absent father put him in charge of the youngsters.

Miles decided to assert his authority: "My project was to discipline Ian. I mean, my sister was at Vassar and my brother was out riding with The King Of Death. Here am I, Mr Conservative — I tried to *save* him."

Without apparently telling Ian, who recalls: "One day I went down to my local hang-out and one of the nurds I normally wouldn't even talk to said 'Hi, I understand you're selling your motor bike. What's wrong with it?' 'My bike? you talkin' 'bout my bike in that disrespectful tone? There's nothin' wrong with it and I'm not sellin' it.' 'Well, *Miles* said it was for sale.' 'WHAAAT?'"

Miles? "I don't remember this story."

Ian wasn't saved. Stewart's hero ran away from home. Jumped on the BSA his mother had bought him and split. At first he just hid in the Armenian sector of the city until his father found him and, instead of demanding that he come home, told his son he worked for the CIA and that he was afraid Ian could therefore become a kidnap target on the loose in Beirut like that. He suggested that Ian should head for England if he really wanted to make a break and actually gave him some money to help him on his way.

The lad may have been taken aback, but he set off. He sold the cycle in Bulgaria and hitched the rest of the way, then settled with some old Beirut biker cronies in the outer London suburb of Ilford.

Another of Miles's ploys as guardian of the Copelands at this period was to cut his siblings' allowance to the bone so that he could play the stock market. He invested well and built up "a nice little wad" some of which he later diverted towards paying for Stewart's college education.

And that's what Stewart had grown up with through to his early teens. It's no wonder he felt such a blank in the middle of that kaleidoscope of crazy color although Miles affirms: "Stewart was a good kid. He got battered by us, but he'd always spring back. He was always positive. Ian would beat him up or Lennie would beat him up and he always came back for more. When he got into something he really got into it. He was very intelligent and he would study."

Stewart's self-portrait remains quite different — a nobody, a dunce: "I can see that Miles and Ian were probably proud of me as older brothers. But they were part of it. I was 'so-and-so's brother'. In Beirut Ian was the talk of the town. Even much later in London I was 'Miles's brother'. The fact is that when I was young I didn't have many friends and the friends I did have used to play 'Ditch Stewart'."

The Beat Boom arrived and Stewart missed it. The Beatles landed at Beirut airport once, and that was it. All he really took to from the weekly blast on World Service was the Kinks whose initial sequence of raw-power hits began with the classic 'You Really Got Me' in the summer of 1964. Apart from the British groups another important omission for Stewart was that he heard relatively little of the most dynamic American music of the day, the soul and R&B variations emerging on the Tamla-Motown, Stax and Atlantic labels, and Bob Dylan's political protest.

But he did begin to play the drums. Ian had borrowed a kit from a friend, trying to grab a spot in one of the pop groups which was attached to each of the Beirut gangs — the brothers aren't too clear whether the band was the Black Knights, who belonged to the Overtakers, or the Dead Ends, who belonged to the Undertakers. Anyway, seeing him practise, Stewart felt something stirring in his blood. He hovered at Ian's shoulder.

Ian says: "Of course, I'd see him waiting there so I'd play longer. You know what brothers are. 'You wanna play do you? Tough, I'm just beginning to get going now.' But actually I was bored with it. Finally Stewart went up to his room and put a couple of books here and a tin can there and battered away. I heard the racket and gave up in disgust."

Once installed on that drum stool there was no stopping him. His father's eyes lit up as he saw the runt of his litter might at last fulfil his own musical ambitions. He told Stewart: "You can play drums on one condition: that you take it very seriously. Then we will get you the best kit and the best teacher." Stewart couldn't have been more eager.

The 'best teacher' wasn't easy to find in Beirut however. The first in a long line through to Stewart's late teens was a guy who his father found playing jazz in a casino. He showed Stewart how to hold the sticks and co-ordinate a few riffs.

It was a lonely business. He hardly played with another musician for most of the next decade. Miles observes: "He was a solo drummer. He had a band of one. His aim was to put in as many shots as possible so that people would be impressed with his double flammadiddle and all that sorta stuff." Ian remembers this cutting no ice with their father, who would badger the boy with "That's all very well, but one thing you're not concentrating on enough is keepin' that goddam beat"

His first chance of a real gig was at the American beach club, a bizarre scene where kids of 12 and 13 would hold all-night parties by Stewart's account: "When I remember what I was getting up to at that early age it ... er ... really shocks me. We were sort of neglected I guess with our parents being such important people. There was a totally decadent, hedonistic society among the kids of the American community."

One night a band that was due to play couldn't track down their drummer, so Stewart got the gig and got his rocks off as reported earlier. A pleasant evening all round.

Lennie, Stewart, Miles and Ian Copeland, 1952.

Drumming was already the most important thing in Stewart's life: "I remember thinking 'I've actually got something I can do that nobody else can do'. At last the complete and utter nobody had something that set him apart and made people notice him. That was a really strong motivation for me."

Unpredictably it had a big effect on Miles too: "Seeing him in a couple of local groups it dawned on me for the first time that show business wasn't so remote from what I wanted. My brother playing in a band Wow!"

In 1966 Beirut suddenly became 'hot' for their father politically and he was given 15 days to leave. Stewart flew to London with his mother, leaving young Miles to complete the Masters degree in the Economics of Underdevelopment he had begun at the American University in Beirut.

Immediately Stewart made a discovery about himself – he didn't speak English. At least only part of the time. Unconsciously the family had evolved a language which dealt with household matters in Arabic and wider affairs in English. It was all words to Stewart, but when he was sent to the London American school for a term he felt a 'culture shock' and hated it.

His parents were sympathetic and sent him to the renowned public (being England that means private) school Millfield in Somerset. In the exotic company of young Asian royalty and British peers Stewart was much happier, although his determined classroom efforts never took him beyond average performance. He did clock up seven O-levels, but when he left Millfield in 1970 it took a term in a 'crammer' to shove him through two A-levels – English History and English Language.

At Millfield he discovered an affinity for horses and soon progressed from mucking out the stables to playing polo for the school team. That took care of the summers. But in the winter it was the traditional upper-class pastime of fox-hunting over the Mendip hills.

Stewart would literally go along for the ride, but once he got too close to the kill and met another ancient custom: "This frightfully English voice called out 'I say young Copeland, come hyar!'. I turned and this thing slapped me round the face. It was the tail, hot from the fox's ass and dripping blood. You're supposed to keep the mark on your forehead 'till the end of the day, but I couldn't stand that. I washed it off and everyone called me chicken on the bus home." Perhaps all this helped him to handle a camel in the Police movie a few years later.

Although he was keeping pretty high-falutin' company, in England there was no way his life could remain untouched by music. Stewart had surfaced in a society where rock was at the hub of life for anyone under 25 – 1967, the year of peace, love and 'Sergeant Pepper's Lonely Hearts Club Band'. His own initiation could not have been more galvanic; the first live gig he went to was the Jimi Hendrix Experience.

Playing guitar with previously unimagined technique and special effects Hendrix had just scored his first two hits 'Hey Joe' and 'Purple Haze,' terrifying sounds in the context of the pop charts. Stewart was overwhelmed: "I was one fried little human being after leaving that place I can tell you! I didn't remember anything after the third number of the set. My mind was a blank for days." The venue was the Saville Theatre and it was the night its owner Brian Epstein, the Beatles' manager, died.

Stewart was shaken, but not stirred into action yet. He allowed himself to be fed back into the education machine for a couple of years until the next phase of his transformation. Meanwhile, there was a brief encounter with Ian who, unwittingly, was about to undergo a revolution himself. Naturally his parents had gone looking for him when they arrived in London and they found him, in his own opinion as well as theirs, "getting nowhere" with his motorcycle mates. He wasn't ready to sink back into the bosom of the family though. He ran for it back to Beirut pausing only to creep into Stewart's St. John's Wood bedroom in the dead of night to borrow £2 and a jacket which was too small for him. He hitched all the way and in a week or two a startled Miles reported that he'd turned up.

Suddenly Ian's rebelliousness wavered for the first time. He agreed to go back to school, a 'special tutoring college', and did take a few English O-levels. It was no use though. So he went to war.

With his father rumbling about sending him to a military academy, Ian outflanked him by enlisting as a private in the US army. The amazing thing was that at last he fitted in — with all the misfits he found in Vietnam. He volunteered for the front line, he was promoted to sergeant at 19, he won medals, he came home a hero. And, at last, Miles 2 and 3 were proud of him.

Ian explains his triumph like this: "Somehow I believed there was no way in hell they were going to get me because this was *my movie*. How could the star get killed?". Exactly.

Stewart could have been next in line for Vietnam when he left school in 1970 and one of the reasons he moved on to an international university in the UK was to avoid the draft. In his own words it was "a fly-by-night clip joint" with abysmal academic standards.

If that was sheer waste, things did start to look up for Stewart when the following year he went to the States for the first time since he was a baby and entered the University of California at San Diego. It was a strange experience for him in that he's always been told he was an American and had the right accent without ever knowing what all this 'land of the free' and 'star-spangled banner' and 'give me a home where the buffalo roam' business was about, except as a theory, a few history books, and *The Virginian* dubbed into Arabic. The mildly uneasy truth was that he felt as much at home and as much a stranger there as anywhere else.

But the university was something special. Stewart's mind went into overdrive to catch up with his lanky body which had lately shot up to his full six feet three. He loved it: "This was a *real* school. Nobel prize-winners giving lectures! They were relayed around the building on TV screens. It was all very invigorating." He majored in Music, then Public Policy and Mass Communications.

"But it wasn't just my grades. I got better at dealing with people too. One moment I was lacking in imagination, the next I was a bright spark, I started thinking and accomplishing. I hate to say it and I would never recommend it because I know of too many casualties, but the only thing it could have been was LSD. I don't take it any more, it did really open my eyes though. Probably an inspiring book might have done it, but it wouldn't have occurred to me to read an inspiring book . . . I discovered a meaning in life.

"It was the littleness and insignificance of myself . . ." for once he struggles for words. "And that I ought to do something about it . . . I suppose. I remember seeing the reflection of my eyes on the lenses of my glasses and

Stewart ready for his first gig at the American Beach Club, Beirut. He's not sure if it was 1966 or 1967.

getting an instant flash, 'Jesus Christ! I'm a complete nobody!', and then going through all the things I could do to be a somebody."

The hint of opportunity arose at the end of his first year from what seemed to be the unlikeliest of sources: Miles and Ian working *together* in a rock band agency and management operation in London and in a position to offer Stewart a job looking after one of their charges on the road.

We had left Miles in Beirut. Loosening his stays a little in his 20s after a few years of college life in the US, Miles says he earned a measure of local fame by staging "wild parties" and this led him to the fringe of the rock scene there. Then, when he finished his MA, he moved to the Copeland HQ in St. John's Wood and soon bumped into a British band called Rupert's People who he'd helped out in the Lebanon. Astonishingly they asked him to manage them, insisting he had the instinct for it despite his inexperience. Another Copeland brother's expectations of himself were about to be turned upside down.

Until then he had been an accepter. He took 'sound' advice towards unorthodox ends: "I'd grown up with the idea that success meant joining a company. Your training, a university degree, was to prepare you to pass the IQ test to get you into the company. And yet I'd always hated that thought: sitting there in a room with hundreds of other people filling in the little blanks on a piece of paper — and my life was going to be judged on *that*!"

Oil was out after all. His father was warning him off the CIA because democratic interference in the agency's activities was limiting it so much it was becoming boring. And Miles had finished his studies of underdevelopment by concluding that the Third World would obstinately refuse to be dragged into the Americanized twentieth century, even by the fierce energies of a Copeland.

"Rupert's people were frankly a godsend. The minute I got the chance to do something that was mine, me, the glory of 'You did it yourself', that was very exciting. I was in the right place at the right time."

Musically he stumbled on what was the beginning of rock's decadent phase, although it was known as 'Progressive' at the time. The rich pickings of the 60s were consumed in a gluttonous orgy which lasted until the punk coronary of '76. Setting himself up as novice manager and agent on the modest foundation of his stock market profits Miles became involved with these Progressive groups, such as Climax Blues Band, Renaissance and Wishbone Ash. His raw instinct looked good for a long time.

He concentrated on America, more than any of his contemporaries, sending his bands on tour after tour. Losses were balanced at first by decent showings in the LP charts. He was soon running quite an elaborate business called British Talent Management, managing several groups, acting as agent for a lot more, in partnership with John Sherry, and working towards tying the strands together into a record company. And by '71 Ian was with him: on the Copeland team for the first time in his life.

Miles reckons Vietnam sorted his brother out: "It gave him a bit of responsibility. There must have been a pride in achievement. He wasn't going to be somebody who'd fail all the time." That is, Ian was ready to shake the money tree.

At least, after a few months he was: "I came back from Vietnam and saw some of the guys I'd been really tight with over there, who'd saved my ass... and at home in the States they were working in the supermarket, living with their wife or girlfriend. I couldn't *relate* to them any more. They were all out of balance, out of synch... weirdness. I was a bit disoriented and I did definitely look back to the family because it made some sense to me."

Acutely aware of the bad atmosphere he would create by favoring his brother, Miles persuaded John Sherry to take Ian on at £5 a week until he had proved himself.

He clicked. That sweet talk he'd always had on the tip of his tongue poured down the telephone line and the office was in fits: "'Hey man, you *gotta* take out this band!' 'Who?' 'Let's see, erm, the Roy Young Band, yay. they're *great*! Yay, and Stackridge too. They *boogie*, boy. They don't just play music, they *entertain*!'"

In a couple of years the Copeland in Sherry Copeland was Ian not Miles.

Stewart served a brief apprenticeship as a roadie with Wishbone Ash and Renaissance, then Miles decided he was ready for grander endeavors. He appointed Stewart 'artistic director' to his hottest protégés of the moment, Cat Iron. Miles's plan was to make them the British Alice Cooper, a rocky horror show. The band included a couple of people who were to prove more important to the Copelands in the long term than the short.

There was Mick Jacques on guitar, later with Stewart in Curved Air. And there was Kim Turner on drums, then only 15, now road manager of the Police. Kim, from Torquay, Devon, is the brother of Martin Turner, Wishbone Ash's bass player.

He recalls Cat Iron's small contribution to rock 'n' roll's decay: "We went out for £50 a night when our expenses were £700 a week. On top of that Miles would pay for our apartment and give us £12 a week to live on, which in those days wasn't bad at all."

The new bright-as-a-button Stewart went out and spent a few thousand on huge amplifiers and a lighting rig and gave the record company the bill. He pressed the by-no-means extrovert group into outrageous costumes and conduct.

Cringing at the memory Kim says: "Half way through the set Stewart, dressed as a policeman, would jump on stage, push everybody off their instruments and shout 'We've had complaints about the noise, it's got to stop'. That was the cue for the strobe lights and we'd all jump on him. Stuffed down his trousers he had this 18-inch black velvet penis. While the other guys pulled it out I'd leap over the drumkit with an enormous pair of shears and chop it off, then it all went black.

"Or that was the idea. The trouble was either I'd lose the shears or Stewart forgot to wear his penis. I think we did it right twice out of ten."

It wasn't the only ordeal Kim went through with Cat Iron. Having a fertile imagination for grotesque publicity stunts, Miles suggested that Kim should marry an 80-year-old woman. Stewart dragged him down to Vidal Sassoon's salon to have his hair cut for the great day. Kim was overwhelmed: "In the middle of them putting this multi-color dye on I fainted and Stewart had to take me to hospital." The caring Copelands cancelled the nuptials.

Soon afterwards Kim slipped out of their ambit for four years when Andy Fraser, former bass player with Free, asked him to join his new band. Kim felt guilty at the

Stewart: "I've got the same ability as Billy Cobham and a million other drummers. It's the imagination that counts. I never heard anything that was beyond me..."

prospect of leaving Miles who had sunk about £10,000 into his career, but Miles's generosity surprised him: "He dropped all claims on me and said 'Hey, if you're a millionaire in ten years let me have a Rolls Royce.'"

In the summer of '73 Stewart had to give up his 'art' for college again. To profitably bridge the gap between London and California he road-managed Joan Armatrading on her first trip across the States.

He moved to Berkeley for his final university year, but finished two credits short of his degree. He became more interested in launching a private enterprise of his own — though with an idea he admits to stealing from Miles. It was a newspaper for social secretaries called *College Event*. He set it up as a free sheet supported by advertizing from the record industry. Neat. But another bug was biting: "I'd got three issues out and was preparing the fourth which would have put the whole operation in the black when I decided to play in a group instead and went back to London."

Again it was Miles opening up the possibilities for him. By mid-'74 he had become manager of Darryl Way, one of the few rock violinists extant. With Sonja Kristina he had founded Curved Air, a heavyish band with neo-classical overtones notable for releasing the world's first picture disc, the 'Air Conditioning' LP, and a 1971 UK hit single called 'Back Street Luv'. He had left the band after their third album, 'Phantasmagoria', and formed Wolf who had failed to cut it.

Miles was shepherding him through the process of developing a new group. He suggested that Darryl might like to check out a certain Stewart Copeland as drummer. Darryl approved and Stewart's career began. The completed line-up played a few gigs superbly named as Stark Naked And The Car Thieves.

Then a financial crisis upset their plans. The VAT-man or similar official was after Curved Air for some thousands of arrears owed. Hastily Miles flung together a tour with most of the original band, featuring Sonja, Francis Monkman (later with Sky) on keyboards, and Florian Pilkington-Miksa on drums. Stewart was shuffled back to tour manager.

It wasn't a great success for him though: "I lasted perhaps two weeks before I couldn't handle working with Darryl as his tour manager. Our relationship was completely changed because the values of a tour manager are not the same as the values of a musician."

A plus was that he rather hit it off with Sonja Kristina and soon they were living together in the first of maybe a dozen flats and houses marking the peaks and troughs of the next few years. Sonja, whose name comes from her Swedish mother, was born in 1949 and has a son, Sven, from her marriage which broke up in the early 70s.

She was probably the key to Air's rarest of comebacks; it actually excited people. Her friendly seduction made the jostling male front rows want to touch without ripping her to shreds. *Deram* Records released a live album from the tour which sold promisingly.

However, with their tax bill paid that was the end of Monkman's and Pilkington-Miksa's interest in Curved Air. So Sonja, Darryl and bassist Phil Kohn were joined by a couple of Car Thieves in Stewart and Mick Jacques. They faced "a grave moral conundrum" – to be settled with heavily loaded dice. Stewart says: "It was 'Now let's see. We're Stark Naked: we load our equipment into the van, drive ourselves up to Nottingham Boat Club, we get paid £50, we load the gear back into the van, drive home and split the £10 that's left five ways. Or we're Curved Air: roadies load the gear, drive, set it up, take it down, drive it home and we get £500 – an entirely different event!'"

The new Curved Air warmed up in Europe, very shaky, with Darryl giving the novice drummer the "death stare". Stewart was in a state, his first real band after ten years practising. "I'd had this suit made which looked totally stupid and I was forgetting what I had to play. I felt I was going to be fired any moment and I was wondering how I'd tell my friends back home."

Then suddenly the band caught fire. The music clicked, the audiences loved them, and they were established as a genuine live attraction. They were even reviewed favorably and Stewart engraved on his memory one critic's comment about "this exciting new find on drums".

In fact fame so tickled his taste buds that he resorted to Machiavellian tactics to establish himself. He began writing letters to the music weeklies using different notepaper each time and disguising his hand: "I think the drummer with Curved Air is amazing" or "I saw Curved Air the other night and I could not believe the dynamic force of their percussionist". At the end of that tour, *Melody Maker* called him in urgent need of an answer to 'a reader's query' (i.e. Stewart's) about what sticks he used. Stewart wrapped up the answer in edited highlights from his life story and landed six paragraphs in the next issue. He couldn't bring himself to tell even Sonja about this chicanery until years later.

Stewart, at 23, was enjoying the constant company of good musicians for the first time and sucking in the experience thirstily. Wherever they moved he and Sonja would set up a 'music room' where anyone who popped round could have a thrash on any instrument available.

Curved Air's spirit and popularity as a live band was unflagging. But in the studio they were effectively scuppered. Their 'Midnight Wire' and final 'Airborne' albums were the outcome of bitter rows with producers which wasted thousands of pounds. Stewart's fledgeling confidence would be tested by comments like "What's that drummer doing? Will somebody tell him to shut up!" from heavy American producers Ron and Howie Albert. The band struggled through, Stewart clung on.

The only consolation for him was that someone had told him about publishing royalties paid to songwriters on each record sold, a whole new concept to him. He went at his guitar like a navvy, hacking out 'songs' with an overspill of energy and not much tune until finally the band accepted a couple and Stewart accepted a £750 advance from Island Publishing.

Through this same period Miles's company, BTM, was undergoing its own crisis. Several of his acts had done well, but his investment was high especially after the record label was launched, and none of the bands could quite make the breakthrough to real stardom and the tidal wave of profit that goes with it.

In mid-'75 he decided his defence would be attack and he set up the 'Star-Trucking' European tour, a package of several name bands with Lou Reed topping the bill and Miles's own Wishbone Ash as chief beneficiaries from the exposure. The gods failed to smile. Reed pulled out, the tour limped through to disastrous losses, and at the same time Miles discovered that by mistake he hadn't given Wishbone Ash their percentage of some thousands of royalties.

BTM was sinking. His bands scurried for the lifeboats: "One of them told me 'You've got no money any more so we don't want to be with you'. My talent didn't mean anything to them. Darryl Way said once 'I expect BTM to keep me in the style to which I'm accustomed'. They all acted as if the company, the *world*, owed them a living."

Miles was in a hole but he refused the obvious course of bankruptcy and paying off his debts at two or three pence in the pound through the Official Receiver. By force of will and the singular kind of trust he can instil in people, he persuaded his creditors not to foreclose and promised he would pay back all the 80,000 dollars he owed. And he reckons he did it within three years even though at first it meant peddling posters in Oxford Street to pay the phone bill.

He was down to a loyal but faltering Curved Air and Squeeze, a then unknown south London R&B band. There was no surrender though. His mind was seething with ideas. For instance, on the floor below his office was a lively bloke called Malcolm Maclaren who was already creating quite a stir with his punk group the Sex Pistols who, in autumn '76, were gaining notoriety by swearing on tea-time TV and being banned by local councils all over the country.

Curved Air were up a blind alley. In debt to the record company, they had to tour constantly to keep any money coming in. Stewart says: "Finally we just played England too many times. It had reached the point where we had no more new material, we didn't have much else in common and there was little prospect of improvement. So we just decided to round off our schedule and leave it at that. Sort of 'Call me if you can think of anything.'"

In mid-December they played Newcastle Polytechnic's end-of-term ball and while they were sitting in the dressing-room after their usual all-out performance to a big crowd, the student social secretary who brought them their thousand pound cheque whined interminably about how it was far too much.

Thinking to cheer them up Phil Sutcliffe, then *Sounds* magazine's North-East correspondent, said there was a great local band called Last Exit playing a late set at a nearby college. Stewart and Sonja said "Why not?" and they all drove over. Last Exit featured a bassplayer/singer with a high, hoarse voice and a certain look. "What's *his* name?" "Sting." Curved Air's drummer had seen the future of Stewart Copeland.

2
STING: TRY PLAYING SCRABBLE WITH HIM

"Did you ever see the Gary Glitter Annual for 1972? Somebody gave it to me as a joke. There are two cartoon stories of how he became Gary Glitter and they're totally separate, contradictory versions of his life. A dual mythology and the reader takes his choice. Very clever. Or perhaps it was an accident. People like Gary Glitter, 'stars', are their own creation and their past life can be a creation too.

"I make no apologies about any lies I've told you — and of course I have told you lies. I dare you to put that in the book You will? Okay. I leave those grey areas because they are painful and I don't want to think about them."

Sting is honest and open enough to tell you that he isn't.

Sting was already 25 when Stewart first set eyes on him. Unknown, unemployed, married with a baby just a month old.

As Gordon Matthew Sumner he was born on October 2, 1951. He is the oldest of four children, with a brother Philip and sisters Angela and Anita. The family lived in Wallsend, an ancient settlement so called because it was the eastern end of the Roman Emperor Hadrian's wall across the north of England.

It's a hard, industrial borough absorbed into the sprawl of Newcastle upon Tyne and suffered the region's withdrawal symptoms as the great heavy industries of coal, engineering and shipbuilding declined after the Second World War. In the 50s Tyneside generally led the nation in pollution, drunkenness, bad housing and unemployment. Despite some improvements it's still a depressed area. The weather in the North-East doesn't change though: windy and cold with no summer to speak of.

The Sumners lived in Gerald Street, a traditional double row of back-to-backs by the river, and they rented their house from Swan Hunter, the biggest shipbuilders in England. Industry on the grand scale like this made everyone feel small as Sting observes: "There was always a huge ship towering over the end of the street."

Sting's father, Eric, had been a fitter in one of the local engineering works when he got married, then he became a milkman and, when Sting was about 6, the family moved a short distance to live in the flat above the small dairy his father ran in Station Road. His mother, Audrey, now an auxiliary nurse, had been a hairdresser, but she had Sting when she was 18 and stopped work for some years while she brought up the children.

The Sumners were never poor, never short of the essentials, but beyond basic material comfort Sting's memories of home are not idyllic. "My family was always on the point of breaking up," he says. "They were always battling. Open, bitter fighting. My parents divorced at last quite recently. But it obviously had an effect on me. Resenting authority.

"As the oldest child I felt very responsible. What would happen to my little brother if my parents split up? Who the fuck would I go with if my mother ran off? Stay with me dad? Nah, I didn't like him very much. Me mother? Nah, she hadn't got any money. And who would take the television?" He laughs ruefully. "I was very concerned about that."

By mid-'81 his brother was working for his father at the dairy, Angela was employed by Dan-Air and Anita was studying for her A-levels.

But the focus of family tension for Sting had shifted from his parents to Phil. Sting says: "We had a big row last year which was very ... unpleasant. Not about me and him basically but ... it's very hard for him to cope with me. Not me personally, I still maintain I'm the same, but me on the television all the time, me on the posters, me the center of attention.

"He's very proud of me I know he is. But it's a younger brother thing. He looks like me and so he's 'Sting's brother' a lot of the time rather than Phil Sumner, which is awful. Things have happened to him such as he's gone to a disco and the DJ's said 'This one is for the Sting poser in the corner'. It must be very hard to take. But what can I do?"

Still, reviewing their whole stormy development he asserts: "None of us are completely fucked up, we're all quite tough and I don't think we regret what happened. I certainly don't. It fed my angst and my ambition."

Of course Sting was a snotty-nosed kid like any other — Newcastle style. The long northern days produced a backstreet life with the children up to all hours playing out: "There was football in the back lane, chasing girls —

18

The Newcastle Big Band: "There was this heavy trip about having the dots written out in front of you, whereas it was really an exercise in how much beer you could drink."

with bricks that is – getting into fights, hanging out around pubs and the chip shop and the Ritz cinema. You used to stop people and ask them to take you into an 'A' certificate. Then there was the children's movies on Saturday mornings." Special treats were football matches and ship launches.

For a while he was barmy about swimming and would spend his 3d at the local baths every night: "My mam was keen on it because it was the only way I got clean". He couldn't be the street urchin all the time though. At 7 he became an altar boy at St. Columba's Roman Catholic church and had to learn the full Latin service as well as looking like an innocent cherub for the duration of Mass.

At school from the start he was always top of the class in English whatever else befell him. "I could write doggerel verse with alacrity, without thinking," he says. At 6 he began what was later to become a fanatical pursuit of 'culture' by reading *Treasure Island* at his grandmother's house. He describes her, Agnes Sumner, as "an extraordinary woman. Brought up nine children – my dad was her eldest. She'd traveled all over the world too.

"There were all sorts of books lying around her home. Copies of *Punch*! Quite an intellectual atmosphere. I read just about everything that came to hand. I think my parents only had the *Evening Chronicle* as far as reading went though I did have a lot of comics, *Superman* and so on, and they were packed with pseudo-scientific information which I loved."

Although he had no shortage of playmates he was obviously drawn to solo pursuits and made his first explorations in music at about the same age as he began reading for pleasure. His earliest "Lawrentian memory", as he calls it, is of sitting under the piano at home listening to his mother play a tango: "She was very good, but she gave it up soon after that. Weird. Due to the break-up of ... I dunno."

He had a go himself almost as soon as he could reach the keys: "I was convinced if I hammered away long enough music would come out – I still am! Anyway music was something I *felt*. Even when I was in junior school I remember running about with new melodies in my head. I always tinkered around even though there was no family background pushing me, no 'Go and practise your scales!'

"Then when I was seven or eight I picked up a guitar

which my Uncle John left with us when he emigrated to Canada. I learnt to play tunes on it quickly and I'd perform for visiting relations."

If that was all sweetness and creativity Sting was about to run into his first real problem: "The trouble was I grew to more or less the height I am now when I was 9! Just under six foot in short trousers. It was ridiculous. I can remember being ... odd. In fact in my first year at grammar school they called me Lurch (*the ponderous butler in* the Addams Family *comic horror TV show*). I was always the one who had to fight the champion from the year above although I was quite peaceful really. At football they stuck me in goal because they thought anybody that size must be impregnable.

"The more I think of my childhood the more I wonder at my acceptance by people now."

Physically grotesque for his age and the victim of childish cruelty because of it, he found he had to work hard to conceal parts of his character and thinking which he feared would lose him the pals he did have: "I never found a truly good friend until my late teens: I mean a friend with whom I wouldn't have to sift through ideas for one they'd understand. I remember one incident vividly. I was watching television with my mate Kevin one night and *Bronco Lane* was on. In this episode Tenderfoot (*hero of another cowboy series*) turned up for a guest appearance. But Tenderfoot was on the other channel at the same time and Kevin said to me 'How can he be on both sides at once?'. I looked at him and I thought 'You're not very clever are you? You're stupid.' I had to explain there was such a thing as film and it wasn't all happening live as you saw it on the TV.

"You had to adopt a common denominator or people would look at you as though you were a bit loony. That went on through adolescence.

"It was the same at school. I was cocky. I knew I didn't actually have to work very hard. In the end of term exams I'd be thirty-eighth out of forty. On paper a C student, but in actuality rather clever which was proved by the 11-plus because it was a very abstract intelligence test. If not for that I would have gone to St. Columba's Secondary Modern school and ended up a juvenile delinquent ... or a milkman or a miner or a shipyard worker. And be unemployed now.

"The teachers were infuriated by me because it was pure native wit and I wasn't using their learning machine at all. They hated me. When the form master heard I was the only one in the class who'd passed he dragged me out in front of them all and said (*enraged colonel's voice*) 'This boy is going to St. Cuthbert's! To a direct grant grammar school! And I think it's a damned disgrace! Sit down boy!'"

'Direct grant' meant that St. Cuthbert's took both the fee-paying children of wealthier parents and others, like Sumner G., covered by local authority grant to the school. His father must have been right on the border line because Sting recalls that he had to pay £15 for the first year and nothing thereafter. The school was a long way from his home in the West End of Newcastle. It was the first major upheaval in his life. As a volatile mixture of arrogance and pained vulnerability Sting wanted a change, although he wasn't sure where it would take him.

Last Exit: "We were very Catholic and yet not very adventurous."

He describes St. Cuthbert's as "very conservative, very reactionary, mainly concerned with football and the saving of souls". He set out to prove that he wasn't going to be 'saved' into conformity: "You had to wear a cap I threw mine away on my first day. 'Where's your cap boy?'. 'I lost it sir'. 'Buy a new one, boy'. 'My mother says she can't afford it.' That completely stumped them and I never did wear a cap. But I had to wear the rest of the uniform. Scarlet jacket, grey trousers, a tie. It set you apart. So did learning Latin, Chemistry and French. Right away I was estranged from the kids I'd grown up with. By the time I'd got home they'd all be playing football in the back lane – with their skintight jeans, brothel creepers and slicked-back hair. Fuckin' hell, I didn't know what I'd passed the 11-plus for"

He soon found out and alchemized his loneliness into energy. The process of wrenching out his neighborhood roots was completed by the family moving to the smart, new Marden Farm Estate near the coast at Tynemouth. His father owned the dairy by then and it was prospering though it always remained on a small scale. As well as taking a mortgage on the house Mr. Sumner bought their first car.

Sting's mother has said of the move: "Gordon never did like the new house. He used to call it a 'little box' and he said that the Wallsend house had much more character. He liked being near the sea though."

Sting was beginning to get a perspective on all of these changes. The importance of social class was bearing down on him and he began to take the steps which seemed required to stay ahead of the system.

"The first thing that went was my accent," he says. "I realized as soon as I got to grammar school that it had to go. I used to *taak like this y'knaa*. I was intelligent enough to see that to get on I had to speak in a non-accent. So I developed this one . . ." It still has traces of the North but you'd be hard-pressed to pinpoint them.

"I don't want to be rooted in Newcastle. I don't want to be known as a Geordie. I've got none of the awful pride. (*Sings the football chant*) 'If you're proud to be a Geordie clap your hands.' Saying Newcastle's a great place. I can't bear that. Newcastle's a shit place. It was a slum from the Industrial Revolution and when they knocked down the old slums they built new slums.

"The only folk hero is Andy Capp and he's one of the greatest anti-heroes of the century. A wife-beating drunkard. I'm too close to Andy Capp to find him funny. Did you know that the bloke who draws the cartoons was born in the next street up from Gerald Street? Anathema. Obscene."

He was in conflict with himself. He wanted advancement and yet he bridled at accepting the orthodox channels to attain it because he couldn't stand bending the knee to authority and couldn't concentrate on dull routine work. He wanted to shake off his background and yet he longed for his old mates and detested the 'snobs' he felt he was surrounded by at grammar school. So he took it out on the teachers and they on him.

"Although I was fairly clever I was never in the coterie of pupils who formed the school establishment, the kind of person that school is designed for," he says sarcastically. "That inner sanctum, the ones teachers love. Usually their parents are teachers themselves or doctors, that kind of middle-class thing. But I was a milkman's son

Sting: "The gestalt of the music is very simple. Three blond-hairs, the macho name, albums that have very camp titles . . . it's very cleverly put together. I'm quite proud of it. It's product. As that I think it's impeccable."

and I always felt I was there by the skin of my teeth.

"I was pretty obnoxious I think. I used my intelligence as a weapon, an affront. I was so bad in the third year that the form elected me captain as a joke. The form master tried to stop it, but they had their own silly democracy and there I was like . . . anti-Christ. The headmaster said 'There is a canker amongst us!' and it was me. We were the top stream, 3A, the cream, and the year after I'd been captain the whole class was demoted, swapped with the second stream.

"Once the whole form was suspended for two days for stealing some equipment from the chemistry laboratory. By the end of term the teachers were refusing to come and give us lessons. I finished that year with an average of 13 per cent in my exams. It wasn't just me. We wanted to destroy. And we did! We were vandals. And this in a very disciplined school. We actually had a master called Father Walsh whose sole purpose was caning. To put the 'fear of God' into us.

"That year I set the record for canings: forty-two strokes. We were caned on the bottom which is undignified to say the least. No matter how tough you are and no matter how determined you are not to cry, three strokes of the cane and you are screaming with agony. It's awful. And I had the record. I'm quite proud of it I suppose. I ended up the only one in the sixth form who wasn't made a prefect. All the rest had these gowns on and there was I – *deliciously* rebellious."

Deliciously. This is probably one of those moments when you should pause and think of the Gary Glitter Annual.

He was dedicated to giving the world and himself a hard time even in areas where he was gifted: "Running was another of the abilities I flaunted at the teachers. I was champion of Northumberland at 100 and 220 yards, but sprinting is something you're born with, there's no strategy involved and not much training.

"I made a breakthrough when I was 8 or 9 and watched another boy running on his toes. I copied him – and that was it! I was very proud of my running until I was beaten into third in the nationals. I didn't want to know after that. Who wants to be third?"

'Plenty of people' is true, but not Sting's answer.

He also wanted to be on top intellectually. He competed with his middle-class fellows in toting around the symbols of avant-garde literature and music which had percolated down to the schools by the mid-60s: the beatnik novels of Jack Kerouac, the new English poetry of Philip Larkin and Ted Hughes, jazz albums by Charlie Mingus and Thelonious Monk. "They were there for the taking," he says. "We'd swap and tape albums though I didn't understand or enjoy that music at the time."

Bob Dylan was certainly one to be seen with: "I was turned on by his poetry like 'Masters Of War', image after image flowing on. The political side of him I took to be about American problems and I didn't feel too close to that. I practised a lot of his songs. I could do all eight verses of 'When The Ship Comes In'." That's a track from his 1964 LP 'The Times They Are A-Changin''".

But, if there was nobody looking, what Sting really enjoyed listening to was the soul on the Tamla and Stax labels and, above all, like most of his generation born in the 50s, the Beatles. They remain the standard by which he judges his art and his career to this day, although he feels rather sadly that they cannot be excelled.

The first live band he ever saw was the Graham Bond Organisation in 1965. They featured Jack Bruce, arguably rock's greatest bass player, who was to go on through John Mayall's Bluesbreakers and Manfred Mann to the heights with Cream. He was the man for Sting all right.

That gig was at the Club A Go Go, Newcastle's best ever venue, a tiny place with a steaming atmosphere which had seen the Animals record an album live with Sonny Boy Williamson and which later, until its closure in '69, presented on their earliest tours such legends as the Pink Floyd and Jimi Hendrix. Like Stewart Copeland, Sting saw him in '67 and remembers him ramming his guitar through the roof of the A Go Go. But the second band he sneaked in for – being under-age yet convincingly large – was Zoot Money And The Big Roll Band with baby-faced guitarist Andy Summers. Zoot honored the establishment with his well-known trouser dropping routine.

His own musicianship continued at a pretty rudimentary level though and strictly behind closed doors. In his early teens he had three piano lessons then gave up because his parents had sold their piano and he found it impossible to learn without practise. However, the guitar achieved the rare feat of bringing Sting and his father close together on occasions.

Eric Sumner could strum along too and on the rare days when he wasn't completely laid out by his hard day which began at five in the morning he would duet with Sting: "We were rivals even then, but there would be brief amnesties. The only comparison would be when I went out with him on his milk round during the school holidays and there was some rapport through sharing the work."

Sting could make even playing an acoustic guitar an act of aggression though: "I'd bury myself in it. I was pretty selfish and isolated. I think that's what made my mum smash my guitar once when I was about 14. I watched her do it. I could have beaten the shit out of her, but I responded to the dramatic nature of the gesture. I just looked at her and made her feel ashamed, then walked out and didn't come back for two days."

Anyway the increasing trend through the 60s for guitarists to adopt the 'heroic' stance with legs spread and agonized grimaces on their faces while playing loud and lousy was turning him off while the genuine and dynamic emotion of Jack Bruce was turning him on. He became fascinated by bass and would play his 45s at 78 to bring out the bottom line.

Then, probably in '66, he took delivery of his first bass: "A friend of mine called Pete Brigham gave me one he'd made. Only two strings worked, the others just buzzed. He and his brother Ken used to make electric guitars out of planks. We used to play the blues in their bedroom. We 'got down' and 'expressed ourselves'. After a year or so the Brigham brothers got into building motor bikes instead and we went our separate ways."

Clearly he was giving no thought to music as a career at that stage. What he craved more and more was 'upward social mobility' – out of Newcastle, out of the working-class. He was never enough of a fantasist to seriously dream of becoming a pop star. He'd rejected sport. His O-levels were unspectacular, five passes in English Language and Literature, Geography, Maths and

Art. What other escape route was there?

His love life. He assailed his girlfriends with all the passion of his class hang-ups as well as his romantic poetic soul. Joking, he'll say: "At 16 I was into girls and music. It was a matter of being the Don Juan of North Shields – as well as the Jack Bruce". But most of his recollections are more melancholy and, he believes, very important to the way he is now. His relationships with two girls in particular he feels changed him from being a destructive to a creative personality.

"I haven't got anything glib," he says. "I'm piecing it together. I think I changed through trauma. The threat of my family breaking up. The threat of isolation. Loneliness has always been there. Which carried on into early sexual encounters. I was very intense as a teenager and I could never really take offhand sex. I was more interested in mind games. Finding a partner for that kind of habit is not easy so I was often frustrated. Especially where I was looking. I still didn't have access to the upper echelons. Seeing a girl with a fantastic body but no brains who I fancied so much . . . I know it was partly the macho environment I was in which told me girls aren't supposed to have brains.

"I wasn't interested in reasons then though. I'd screw'em and be strangely unsatisfied. I used to get girls 'pregnant' all the time," he snorts ruefully. "'What shall I do? Buy a bottle of gin and have a bash? Let her have it? Oh fuckin' hell' And then she'd come on after six weeks of torture.

"I'd always be looking for the right one. I suppose we all are, but . . . I needed . . . a middle-class girl is all I mean. I felt . . . locked out. I had this beautiful girlfriend called A who was very working-class, an absolute goddess. I couldn't believe that I had this thing, I owned this thing. Not very bright, but a very lovely person. And I wanted her to be something she wasn't.

"I was constantly bringing her books to read. 'This is *Howard's End*, its by E.M. Forster and it's a really good novel.' Next day she'd come back and say 'Well, I read the first page and I thought it was boring'. She was reading things like *Jackie* and *Boyfriend* and I wanted to strangle her. She was ignoring great art which would be useful to her and demeaning herself with crap.

"Eventually I got her pregnant and she miscarried which was a terrible trauma for her – and me. Then I met this girl B who was the daughter of a headmaster. This chick had actually read Jean-Paul Sartre. Fuckin' hell, I was fascinated. B had access to whole realms I'd longed for and I left A in the lurch.

"It took a long time. A was very close to me and to my mother. There was a great tearing apart. At the same time her mother contracted cancer of the throat and died very quickly. That was going on in the middle of my attraction to B. A was going through hell and within a year she was destroyed. As soon as her mother died she went to work in a mental hospital as a help and I think that was one of the things that . . . the despair you see in a mental hospital. She killed herself."

Adept as he is at subtly showing himself in a fairly shining light Sting draws no shred of self-aggrandisement out of this. He makes no resonant speeches about how grieved and guilty he felt. He just stumbles on: "I . . . never forgave myself. I know that if I'd stayed with her ultimately I would have destroyed her anyway because of my ambition.

"The affair with B went on for about three years and ended disastrously in another very creative phase for my angst. She left me for someone else. I'd never had that happen to me before. Almost a repeat of what I'd done to other people. So I learnt. It was painful because I had friends in common with her new bloke. I couldn't get away from it. It was humiliating.

"Songs like 'The Bed's Too Big Without You' are rooted in that period. It's fairly close to the A episode of being a partial cause of suicide. If I have to conjure the feeling to write a song of despair I go there. You know I felt deep grief at what happened to A, but I used it then and I'm using it now. When you look at it it's quite horrid.

"But I did love those girls. One very physically, the other intellectually".

Sting left school in summer, 1969, hoping to go to university if his A-levels were good enough. Meanwhile he filled in time making money as a bus conductor in Newcastle, a job which, oddly enough, he was able to enjoy as a short-term proposition because of its public performance quality: the conductor very much in charge of the situation – strutting up and down the aisle with a smile, a joke, a song, dramatic scenes with drunks and fare dodgers.

His A-levels were mediocre passes in Economics, Geography and English and that threw his plans into confusion. The 'clearing house' computer system for getting into university at the last minute, tried to find an undersubscribed course which would take him. Sting became hopelessly tangled in the administrative net.

He explains: "I was accepted by Warwick University to do English and by Lanchester Poly to do something bizarre like, er, Computer Science – at the same time They're both around Coventry so I went down there and I was darting between one and the other trying to sort it out. My grant didn't come through. I was lost. Administratively and academically nowhere. Drunk all the time. Away from home, completely out of it, not knowing where I was.

"Eventually I decided I'd go back home and do something I really wanted to do. Except that I hadn't a clue what that was. I needed time to rethink."

Altogether Sting must have had a thoroughly bruised ego. He was back living with his parents like the stay-at-home Geordie he has caricatured. For the time being his insecurities were on top: "It was 'What the hell am I going to do with my life?'. I was playing music. I'd been writing songs for years. I knew I had talent. But I needed . . . some kind of institution to support me."

He did a year on the building sites and the dole, enjoying the labor but daunted by visions of himself pot-bellied and wrecked in twenty years time. He donned a suit to get a job at the Inland Revenue with the high rank of Executive Officer, but he reckoned they might as well have bought another adding machine for all the scope he was given: "There was one case where I found a way of working out the computations for allowances on life insurance more easily and the head guy came down and told me I couldn't do it. 'But it's simpler this way'. 'No.' A brick wall. That was it for me."

He applied for a place at Northern Counties Teacher Training College on the outskirts of Newcastle and was accepted for the autumn 1971 term. He enrolled on the

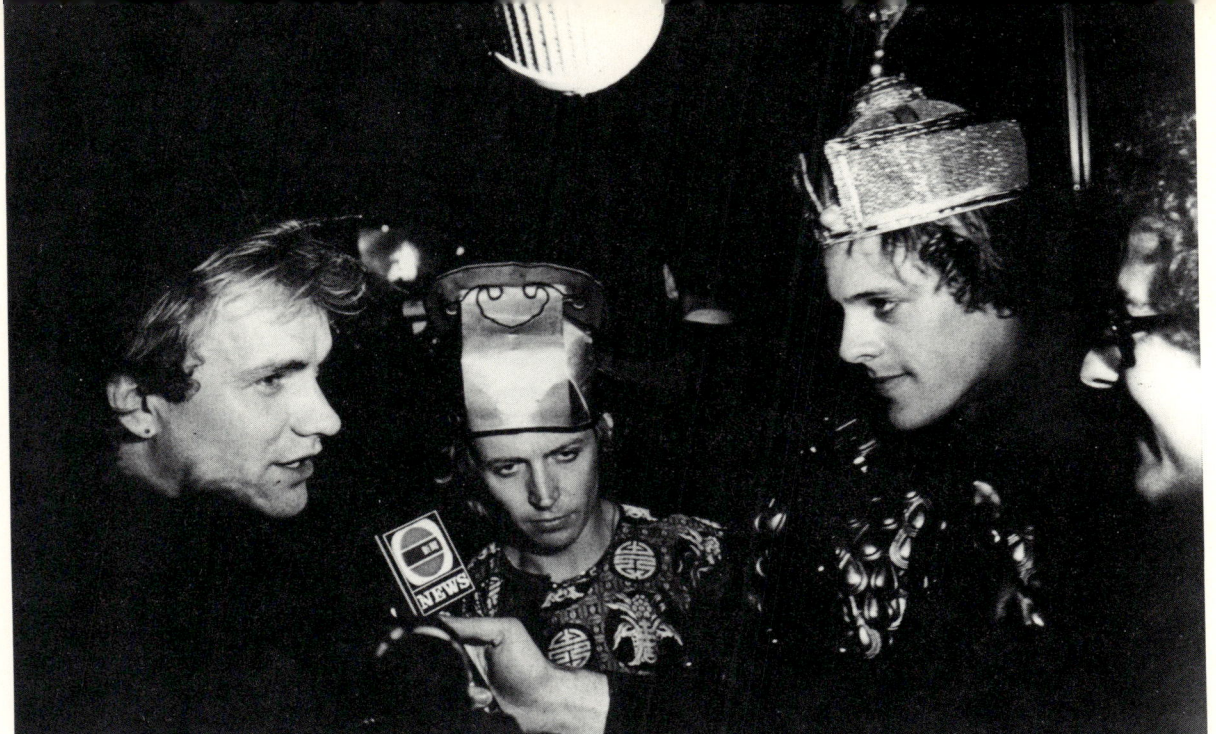

English Bachelor of Education course, but soon lowered his sights to a more comfortable Teachers Certificate in English and Music.

He did have some genuine feeling for teaching despite his loathing of school: "I saw a limited area where I could influence people for the better, create an environment of learning opposite to the way I was taught." On the other hand he didn't think it would be too demanding: "I said 'Right, I'm in an institution where I don't have to work that hard and I can play music'. I needed that kind of womb.

"And that's where I met Gerry Richardson."

It's probably fair to say that Gerry Richardson is one of the three most important people in Sting's life — the others being Frances Tomelty and Stewart Copeland. Gerry was born in Leeds in 1950 and was always destined to be a musician. He sang in choirs and was encouraged to play piano by school teachers who were active in the local jazz scene themselves. At Northern Counties he was in the year above Sting, studying English. Gerry, a keyboards player, had already formed a band playing jazz with a sprinkling of Joe Cocker-style soul. His girl singer told him about this bass player, Gordon Sumner, she'd seen doing spots as a soft-rock balladeer at the folk club. He was singing James Taylor numbers.

"I went along and thought he was all right," says Gerry. "But frankly I didn't give a toss about Sting's bass playing until we got talking and I discovered he knew a drummer who owned a van and a PA. That's what I really wanted, so I sacked my bassist and drummer and we formed this new line-up called Earthrise."

He found Sting rather reluctant to sing at that stage and at first his only vocal was on a cover version of the old Ashton, Gardner and Dyke hit 'Resurrection Shuffle'. The two quickly became close friends and spent their time trying to impress people with flashy jazz techniques while groaning at the foul noises coming from Earthrise's horrible horn section.

Gerry and Sting were serious about it all right. On the other hand they were obviously going nowhere. At random they explored other musical avenues. Gerry filled in on bass with the Phoenix trad jazz band. When he left, the post passed to Sting. It was no great shakes — except that it gave him the name to launch a thousand front pages.

The wacky Phoenix lads had a rule that every member should be known by a nickname. Plain Gordon Sumner turned up wearing the now legendary black and yellow hooped sweatshirt. Trombonist Gordon Soloman thought "He looks like a wasp", then "Ah *Sting*". And it stuck. At last Sting could dump that rotund, clumsy 'Gordon' he'd always detested.

So Sting played the New Orleans standards of immortals like Satchmo and Kid Ory, even the dross ballads like 'She Wears My Ring' the band had to include to break the ice at working men's clubs. It seems he'd pressed the 'Hold' button on all the ambition and frustration which had goaded him through his youth. He sat back and soaked up experience in a circle of musos much older than himself. He had a good time.

And he began to get noticed. Soon the well-respected River City Jazzmen invited him over from the ramshackle Phoenix. Then somebody asked if he would like to join the Newcastle Big Band and he turned up for a rehearsal.

The band's founder and conductor, all-round entrepreneur and culture activist Andy Hudson, was struck by Sting's arrival: "To begin with he couldn't really read music and after that first session our lead sax man Nigel Stanger told me 'I can't play with that new bassist. You'll have to get rid of him'.

"Well, you can't run a 16-piece democratically. I listened to people and ignored them. Sting had a quality of enthusiasm which is instantly recognizable. He would nick the parts and take them home to study. Another thing about him was the reliability factor. In five years of working with him he was never late. That's important."

The band was a bleary focus of many a drunken Sunday lunchtime in the University Theatre bar and Sting came to terms with another style, another repertoire:

Duke Ellington, a cacophonous version of the Beatles' 'Hey Jude' and, when matters got totally out of hand, 'The Laughing Policeman'. An album preserving some of these raucous renderings was recorded at the Theatre and on a visit to Pau, France. It's more comic than classic, but copies have changed hands for £30 since Sting became the Face of the 80s.

From '71 to '74 Sting was simultaneously in all these outfits. In effect he was living and working in a 'community' for the first time — the community of music — and he threw himself into it without restraint. For instance, he became an active member of the Musicians Union, supporting Andy Hudson's campaign to take the Newcastle branch out of the hands of the employers, the professional band leaders.

They scored one victory when some of the old fogies tried to stop a school for young musicians which Andy had set up. The objection was that the pupils "might not be union members". But the Big Band cohorts duly packed the meeting and kept the course open to allcomers.

In fact Sting attended some of the classes. For a while he was utterly preoccupied with improving his technique on bass. He would practise eight hours a day, even during lunch breaks at college when he and Gerry slipped away to the music room for a jam with Sting playing an otherwise neglected double bass — learning the skills he now uses on that spike-like electric upright on stage with the Police.

However, this devotion was leading toward a certain self-knowledge rather than earth-shattering virtuosity. With much affection Sting says of the Big Band: "It was a lovely time for me because I was young and energetic and I could kid myself I was playing with serious musicians. But I wasn't! There was this heavy trip about having the dots written out in front of you whereas it was really an exercise in how much beer you could drink. They all had jobs behind desks and their one delinquency was music.

"The idea of being a muso seduced me for a while and it didn't do me any harm. Really my talent lies elsewhere though. I haven't got the right shaped hands." They're rather thick and stubby-fingered. "I reached the limit of my instrumental ability. For me playing is the means to write songs."

Committed as he was, music didn't occupy his every waking hour. Pursuing his 'rethink' he became involved in political activities at his college and declared himself a Marxist. The doctrine was an exact contradiction of all the longing for middle-class status, culture and money he had experienced at grammar school.

It wasn't just hot air either: "I read all the books. I went out on forays against the National Front when they had a candidate at South Shields in a General Election in '74. I used to drive the bus for the college Socialist Society. In fact when I was on the demo outside Durham jail against the force-feeding of the Price sisters (convicted IRA terrorists who went on hunger strike) I actually got my first front page! I was on the cover of *Red Weekly*, looking very much the Trotskyite with a beard and placards all round me: 'Stop force feeding! Political status now!'"

Certainly Sting has become much more 'moderate' since then — otherwise there'd be no collaborating with the Copelands — but he still describes himself as at least a socialist and votes Labour. He scorns the street politics he used to take part in and dismisses Marxism as "unworkable". Perhaps the politics of ambition have won. Or you might argue that it would have been hypocritical of him to remain a Marxist when he became wealthy.

Nonetheless, with the knowledge of circumstances in Northern Ireland he has gained through his wife Frances, who comes from the beleaguered Catholic neighborhood of Andersonstown in Belfast, he does have some understanding of political violence: "I *know* that if I'd been born in Andersonstown or the Bogside I'd be a member of the IRA a) for my own protection b) because I'm that sort of person c) because there is a historical and current situation which is intolerable. I abhor terrorism. It's in all of us though."

At last he left home. In 1974 he went to share a flat with an actor called Newton Wills in Jesmond, the student/young middle-class district of east Newcastle: "By then I wasn't that bothered about leaving home. In fact I had to. There was no room for me in that house. It was kind of exploding."

Finishing his course a year earlier, Gerry had been in Bristol earning good money with a club band, but they were sacked and he returned to Newcastle just as Sting was passing his exams. They decided to go all out to put together the group they dreamed of. They'd both seen their messiahs and they knew what they wanted: jazz-rock.

For a couple of years in the mid-70s every young hopeful with pretentions to musicianship was looking to the pyrotechnic skills of bands like Tony Williams' Lifetime (Jack Bruce again), Weather Report and Return To Forever. Sting had had the humbling experience of supporting the latter at Newcastle Polytechnic in the Big Band: "We were the usual drunken melée and shuffled off with our music stands, then on came Return To Forever and ... Jesus Christ! My eyes were out here! Supergroup? They were gods!

"And Stanley Clarke on bass, outrageous. It changed my whole way of thinking. There was a period when bass playing seemed to erupt with Clarke, Jaco Pastorius and in England Colin Hodgkinson of Back Door. The whole tendency was to come out front and be much more aggressive instead of trundling away in the background."

Setting high technical standards Gerry and Sting found themselves turning to older musicians in guitarist John Hedley (replaced after a year or so by Terry Ellis) and drummer Ronnie Pearson, formerly with Back Door himself, a Lancastrian who claims to have once taught Ringo Starr. Sting took nearly all lead vocals with occasional excursions by Gerry and Ronnie.

And this was Last Exit. From a Wednesday night residency in the tiny upstairs room of a pub called the Gosforth Hotel they proceeded to shake Newcastle. They played their Chick Corea cover versions and amazed people not used to such speed and dexterity. But what really warmed their audiences was the unpredictable mixture of soul material such as Fleetwood Mac's 'I Need Your Love So Bad' and Bill Withers' 'Friend Of Mine' with moody melodic compositions by Sting and Gerry.

Soon they had an astonishing repertoire of 70 num-

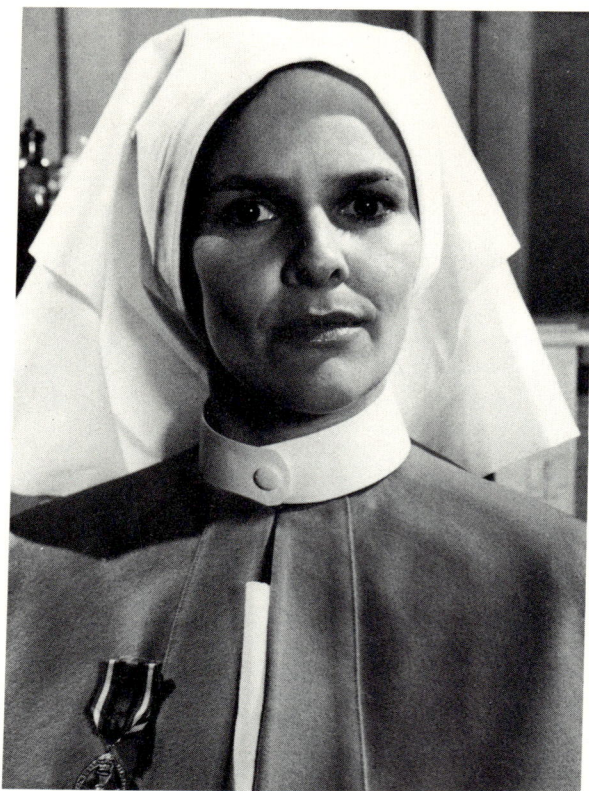

Frances Tomelty as Sister Milroy in the BBC dramatisation of *Testament of Youth*.

bers so that there was a different set every week drawing the regulars back. As Gerry says: "The breadth of material was ridiculous commercially, but it was policy for me and Sting. We believed in being eclectic and that class will out."

Significantly they began another residency in Back Door's hometown, Blakey Ridge on the Yorkshire Moors. It was a declaration of solidarity: they too would "do it from the North-East". What they possibly overlooked was that Back Door were failing despite enormous expenditure by Warner Brothers on their four albums.

But in Newcastle Last Exit's regular gigs at the Gosforth and the University Theatre bar, were the event of the week. Although there was never any room to dance, their superb funk was capable of jerking every sinew in your body, while their quiet moments could move you deeply. An impassioned love song by Sting called 'I Burn For You' beginning *a capella* could stun the bar-room rumpus to wide-eyed silence in five seconds.

Yet the overall atmosphere was fun and friendliness symbolized by that Bill Withers signature tune and expressed through Sting's easy, almost joyful, manner between numbers. Simply, Last Exit were loved. But, as they were to realize over the next couple of years, only on Tyneside.

In autumn '74 Sting had started work teaching five to nine-year-olds at St. Paul's First School in Cramlington, a new town just north of Newcastle. He was the only member of Last Exit with a day job. During this period Sting shared a flat with John Hedley, then with Gerry.

A couple of months later the band landed a gig at the University Theatre Christmas show, a musical written by veteran pop writer Tony Hatch called 'Rock Nativity'. Acting and singing as the Virgin Mary was an Irish girl called Frances Tomelty, then 27, the daughter of well-known film actor Joseph Tomelty. However, she didn't take to Sting immediately.

Frances recalls: "We'd go back to where I was staying and the deal was I'd make the cheese on toast while he'd serenade me with his guitar."

"Music was very much a part of the seduction process," Sting chuckles. "It still works even with a large group of people. Serenade all these birds and they want to deliver their bodies to you."

When the show's run ended Frances went back to London and the two began more than a year of commuting to see each other at weekends, though sometimes this would be in Edinburgh or Sheffield as Frances got work in other provincial theaters. She also had a part in a children's TV series, *No Place To Hide*, and is still recognized on the street for that rather than any of her major roles since.

At first Frances didn't become involved with the band's progress, but Last Exit had enough distractions not to notice they were only treading water.

There were support spots with lesser touring bands who passed through such as Osibisa, Zzebra, Colosseum, and a bizarre project, the orchestral 'Tubular Bells' which by a freakish coincidence featured Andy Summers in the Mike Oldfield role on guitar – he and Sting didn't meet.

They entered the notoriously naff *Melody Maker* rock contest's North-East heat and blew it. The often errant John didn't show up so they improvised a couple of numbers and came third out of 30 with only two to go through. They auditioned for a Tyne-Tees TV show called *The Geordie Scene* which packaged a star name with a local band. The producer said: "Great! But the kids won't be able to cope with your rhythm changes. Sorry."

In the summers they'd take off. First it was San Sebastian, a huge jazz festival which presented greats like Ella Fitzgerald and Oscar Peterson on the same bill as unknowns like themselves. The Big Band were there too, sponsored by the Spanish Tourist Board after some wheeler-dealing by Andy Hudson, but relegated to the market square for the pleasure or otherwise of the shoppers. Last Exit actually made it on the main stage in the velodrome in front of 3,000 people and were such a hit that Spanish TV broadcast one of their songs.

Then it was a sea cruise. Ronnie and Terry had done the Palm Court bit on the liners before and it looked like fun in theory. Gerry says: "We were signed on for two weeks holiday relief, but the problem was Ronnie organized it and anything he did he wanted to be brilliant whereas I just wanted to keep people happy and Sting wanted a holiday. It was a ghastly compromise. Sting only knew about three standards, we were always too loud and Ronnie was unhappy. I hated that period because I hate acrimony and there was a lot of it about."

It erupted more than once between Gerry and Sting back on shore, notably in a domestic scene which saw Gerry break a plate over Sting's head and Sting pour a bowl of hot soup over Gerry. They can't remember what started it, but they do recall that the next phase was a row over which was the worst offence. They agreed to settle it by Sting breaking a plate over Gerry's head and Gerry pouring soup over Sting — or perhaps they cracked up before it went that far.

If all this was pretty aimless they were also applying themselves to the serious business of recording demos. From February '75 to January '76 they spent a lot of time at Impulse Studios, Wallsend, only a few hundred yards from Sting's old home. The owner, Dave Wood, allied with Andy Hudson in trying to promote the group.

They released a single of Gerry's 'Whispering Voices' sung by Sting and then a nine-track 'album' on cassette because it's cheaper than vinyl when it's a matter of only a few hundred copies. The title was 'First From Last Exit' and the songs were Sting's 'We Got Something', 'Carrion Prince', 'On This Train', 'Oh My God', 'Truth Kills' and 'Savage Beast' with Gerry's 'I Got It Made' and 'Whispering Voices' and a Terry Ellis instrumental. In fact Dave has several tracks on a master tape he keeps in a local bank vault because when he suggested he might put them out as an 'Early Sting' album to 'recoup his investment' there were immediate legal noises from Miles Copeland.

Last Exit certainly never did themselves justice in the studio and there is a stiffness and sterility about some of these recordings which had no part in their live performance.

Dave Wood has another fascinating relic on his shelves: Sting's first venture into reggae. Bob Marley had surely reached his ears through the 'Natty Dread' and 'Live' LPs and 'No Woman No Cry' hit single in '75, but it was Dave who proposed that Last Exit take a shot at it skank-style. His father had just returned from a holiday in Barbados with a pile of records and Dave thought a song called 'Put On Your Wings And Fly' might give them the chance to be early on to the bandwagon.

The strange thing was that, according to Gerry, Dave wouldn't let Sting sing it at first and eventually recorded it with him in duet with Ronnie. Gerry's verdict: "It was awful". It was never released and Sting's budding sympathy with natty rhythms was further rebuffed when Ronnie refused to play a reggae song he wrote for Last Exit, 'Let Me Do It To You'.

Add all this up and the picture is of hectic action, no reaction. Record company A&R talent scouts always said the demos were "good but . . ." Last Exit's hopeful career was stagnating and perhaps Sting was too, despite his current impression of himself as constantly fired by ambition.

For instance, Frances clearly remembers that when they were getting to know each other Sting presented himself to her as a keen, young teacher who also played music, rather than the rampant, rising pop star. His job fascinated him. He delighted in being different to all the hardline schoolmasters he'd known, making a point of turning orderly classroom procedure upside down. He brought the children boxes of musical instruments and played and sang with them.

Ever sure of his abilities he asserts: "I did teaching well, very well. It was useful experience in not being nervous in front of a number of people. I learnt to entertain delinquents for an hour. Same as now. I learnt timing, rapport, how to talk to kids without making them think you're a jerk. The trouble was a lot of them had never really been talked *with*. Well, the job of a teacher is to be human."

If he was close to 'settling down', events were to give his ambition a sharp kick. Frances and Sting married on May 1, 1976, at St. Oswins Roman Catholic Church in Front Street, Tynemouth. While Sting has his religious doubts he always seems to think in terms of the existence of some form of 'God', and in any case he has a strong feeling for the church ceremony: "I couldn't stand the sterility of an off licence. No, what do I mean? A registry office. I wouldn't have felt married."

And, with their troth plighted, a new dynamic came into his life. Sting and Frances combined had a formidable, urgent energy, especially when she became pregnant. Frances says: "I was 28. I *needed* a baby. My whole self was telling me it was the right time. Our careers didn't come into that side of it at all. But there was no way I could have settled in Newcastle. I'd lived in London before and it held no terrors for me — although perhaps it did for Sting."

Gerry reckons: "There was a crucial change in Sting because of Frances. I think she's pushed him like fuck . . . although he has always been an incredibly competitive bloke — try playing Scrabble with him"

Of course the bride and the groom's best friend are classic rivals in the early stages of any marriage, but Gerry and Frances agreed about the band's prospects. Gerry's "We might as well be big in Hong Kong as Newcastle" was echoed by her "Last Exit have to get out because in five years they will just be old men the local kids come to for tips on how to play."

Temporarily sidelined from acting, Frances turned to helping the band. She advised Sting on stagecraft: "When I first saw Last Exit he used to look around a lot. He thought he was drawing the audience in, but I knew it diffused concentration and made him look nervy and awkward. I said 'Be still'." He was and it worked. These days he doesn't look at you, you look at him.

She also took their latest demos on another round of the record companies in London: "It's quite soul-destroying for a band to do that themselves. 'Listen. This is my art.' It might have been an advantage to have me

there able to joke and flirt with the A&R men — and very pregnant too." Even so, no takers.

Pressured by the positives of their music and their ambition and the negatives of constant rejections the power struggle of the band was changing. Essentially Gerry's group had become Sting's. "I'm a usurper," Sting laughs. "Should I hide my light under a bushel? I ain't that sort of a person."

If Gerry ever felt a twinge of resentment eventually he rationalized it: "To get on we had to shove Sting to the front. I knew Sting was going to be a star. He developed this incredible relationship with the audience. He was bright, wrote good songs, had a brilliant voice. And of course there's this incredible charm. Everyone who knows him likes him."

Sting sees the shifting of their deep personal and musical relationship like this: "Gerry's always been very brotherlike. The bad side as well as the good side. Always over my shoulder. I love him dearly, but I'm very much into rivalry and we are *still* rivals.

"I always envied Gerry his musical upbringing, the choir at Leeds Cathedral and all that, even though I'm a much more natural musician than he is. It flows out of me whereas he had to struggle to write a tune. When we lived together in competition as songwriters his frustration was so apparent, but there was nothing I could do about it. I'd come out with about three songs a week and he hated it I'm sure."

But Gerry was right behind the change in Last Exit's style produced by these tensions. The shades of Back Door and Return To Forever faded. They were becoming a pop group.

Fans used to a plethora of polyrhythms suddenly found themselves singing along to Sting's easygoing 'Don't Give Up Your Daytime Job': "That was the most overt example of my crass desires. I played it to Gerry and he said 'Christ, that sounds like a hit!'. I wanted to play accessible music far more than I wanted to re-create Art Blakey's Jazz Messengers — there'd been a lot of that in Last Exit, conservative inertia. We were very catholic and yet not very adventurous."

'Don't Give Up Your Daytime Job' was a self-mocking piece which Sting introduced after he'd done just that. He resigned from St. Paul's and from teaching in the summer of '76 despite the imminence of Joe's birth in November, a startling gamble for one who had never exactly been a Bohemian for all his ups and downs. As he says: "Frances was already into that style of life. Anyway it was a relief. I'd had two jobs for two years and I was fucking knackered.

"'Daytime Job' had its humor, but it came out of frustration, shut out by a non-caring régime. One of the biggest influences the Sex Pistols had on me was that they were destroying something which had held me back. I was older, a much more sophisticated musician and a more mellow person than Johnny Rotten or Sid Vicious, but I could relate to that anti-establishment feeling. The energy and aggression — hatred!"

The Sex Pistols. Punk. Last Exit? They were aiming for new heights of intelligent, musicianly, melodic pop when the nation's youth was engrossed in spikey hair, bondage pants, gob and anarchy.

Clues to the quality of Sting's material at that time lie in the Last Exit songs he's adapted for the Police, such as 'The Bed's Too Big Without You' and 'So Lonely', which began life as Exit's 'Fool In Love'.

He explains how a couple of others evolved into their present form: "'Bring On The Night' was originally called 'Carrion Prince'. I got the title from a Ted Hughes poem, *King Of Carrion*. It was about Pontius Pilate and so was the song originally. Now it's about Gary Gilmore! I didn't realize it until I read *The Executioner's Song* by Norman Mailer, the story of Gary Gilmore. 'Bring on the night/I couldn't stand another hour of daylight.' Gilmore's death wish. This very abstract thing I wrote fits this incredible true story. I sing it with him in mind and it's got to be the theme song if they make a movie of his life.

"Actually another Ted Hughes poem called *Truth Kills Everybody* gave me the idea for 'Truth Kills' in Last Exit which became 'Truth Hits Everybody' on 'Outlandos D'Amour'."

Last Exit were close to the edge. At last someone in London expressed an interest. Carol Wilson of Virgin Music Publishing took such a shine to them that she persuaded a battalion of company luminaries, including Virgin boss Richard Branson, to journey up to Newcastle and see them support Alan Price at the City Hall.

But ... Sting: "Disastrous. Soundchecking as the audience came in, one mike on drums. Not very auspicious." Like a French Revolution jury the Virgin contingent gave the thumbs down and dropped the guillotine on their hopes again. Except that Carol Wilson wouldn't wear it. She offered Exit a publishing deal regardless. The contract was posted to Frances who showed it to Gerry. He recalls: "She said 'Read this'. I got about half way down the page, but it didn't make any sense to me."

So they signed. They were ready to clutch at any gesture of belief in the group by then. Sting had no idea that he was storing up trouble for himself and he accepted the legal minimum publishing royalty of 50 per cent with five annual 'options' — one of those words which means less in a contract than it does in conversation: "I trusted that meant *mutual* options, that I had as much freedom to pull out as they did. That was my stupidity." He was held to 50 per cent when many major writer/performers are on 80-90 per cent. Sting's lawyers were still fighting the case in spring '81.

However, in that punk mid-winter, all Carol Wilson knew was that she was trying to score a record deal for an obscure and unfashionable talent. She did what she could. She booked a 'showcase' gig at Dingwalls club in London, one of the cooler places to be seen.

Phil Sutcliffe traveled down with Last Exit and watched them flogging their guts out in front of two dozen laid-back observers. The resulting three-page *Sounds* feature seemed like some kind of breakthrough, and Carol gave them time to record some fresh demos at Pathway studios on the same trip. So they pointed roadie Jim's Transit northwards again on a charge of considerable optimism.

They had decided — they would move to London and damn the torpedoes. It was unanimous, definitely. Their faith, confidence and unity seemed to have attained a new strength. They had already announced their farewell Newcastle gig at the University Theatre on January 6 when one December night Stewart Copeland wound down from a Curved Air set by watching Last Exit at St. Mary's Teacher Training College.

3

WE'RE GONNA PLAY SOME PUNK NOW

When Stewart first saw Sting playing with Last Exit up in Newcastle, Curved Air were coming to the end of their last tour. "Watching Sting I immediately identified with him as being a young man in an old band – a vibrant force surrounded by fuddy duddies. I remember thinking 'I wish they'd get on with it'. I had the feeling it was the people around Sting who were holding him back."

Curved Air played their final gig just before Christmas 1976 and Stewart immediately got down to sorting out what he wanted to do next. He was aware that punk rock was starting to make an impact and he wanted to be a part of it. Punk was also getting more visible. At the end of the year the Roxy Club opened up in a dingy basement in Covent Garden and provided an immediate focus for the new bands and their fans.

Stewart's first confrontation with punk had come earlier at a party in the large apartment he shared with brother Ian. By this time, Ian had built up the Sherry Copeland Agency as far as he wanted to take it and was preparing to move to America and start up again where there was more scope for expansion.

"We'd invited everyone we ran into to this wild party," remembers Ian. "There was Al Stewart and all his crowd there and then the Sex Pistols and some other punks turned up. They were a bit of a novelty at that time.

"Later on this fight developed downstairs and I went down to sort it out. 'There's a problem: this guy keeps putting on punk records and we want to play the Average White Band'. The single this guy was trying to put on was 'Blank Generation' by Richard Hell (one of the first singles on Stiff Records). This punk finally convinced me to let him play it. I said 'OK, after the next James Brown record'. So he put it on and all the punks went crazy while the rest of the room looked on in amazement. The next day it was still on the turntable and Stewart and I came down and cleaned up the house to the sound of 'Blank Generation' and we fell in love with it; it was a great record."

Stewart quickly realized that punk was much closer to his own rock and roll instincts than anything he'd done with Curved Air. "It certainly seemed like it was worth talking about. And when some of the values started sprouting out they immediately made perfect sense to me. When I'd been arguing with Darryl Way or Mick Jacques over musical principles of 'shall we do it this way or that way'; after all those arguments I'd have with producers that were thrust upon us; all those values which were native to my taste I had to discount because nobody around agreed with me. So I just stopped arguing.

"My taste in music is for loud guitar and exciting stuff. I didn't want just to be a good back beat (which ironically is something he had to learn with the Police). But everyone was talking about laying back and Curved Air's tour manager's favorite group was Hall and Oates and he was always playing us tracks and saying that we should try something like that . . . (he imitates a somnolent laid back wail). It got to the point where I was actually embarrassed about my Jimi Hendrix collection."

Once Curved Air was finished Stewart was determined to form his own band without delay. "I actually had the name 'The Police' before there was anybody but me in the group I worked on the concept and everything before I found anybody to play in it."

There was one false start before Stewart decided to recruit Sting, prompted by Sonja who saw how he might fit Stewart's plans. "There was this group called the Rockets who changed their name for one gig because I was jamming with them. And I thought that maybe I would use them. The guitarist was a pretty good singer. For a while they were into the idea but I decided that they didn't have enough out of the ordinary. In fact they'd actually changed their name to the Police before I'd made up my mind and they had another gig booked under that name. So I said 'Hold on, wait a minute'."

A few days into 1977 Stewart rang Sting (having got the number from Phil Sutcliffe) and asked him to come down and play with this band he was getting together. What he didn't know was that Sting was coming down to London in January anyway. "I thought my gift of the gab had persuaded him to leave his group and his home and I thought 'great', but it turned out he was going to move down anyway."

In fact Sting was under the impression that he was coming to London to set up Last Exit on the club circuit. "We'd all agreed to do it but I was the only one who did I'd made my plans, I'd left my steady teaching job and there they were – the professional musicians – scared to

37

actually make the move."

Sting, Frances and Joseph spent the next few weeks sleeping on the floor of Frances's friend Pippa Markham, an agent who has handled all their acting careers (including Joseph's), waiting for the rest of Last Exit to follow. "I wrote a letter to the band saying 'Look, I'm totally committed to Last Exit but I'm committed to the Last Exit who said they wanted to make it, who said they were coming to London. Come down or the group's finished'. Gerry did come down, God bless him; the others didn't.

"It was a funny time, 1977. So much was swept away by the Sex Pistols and in a way I think Last Exit would have been too. Except that before I'd felt very comfortable about Last Exit's chances. I thought I had the hit songs in me. But I had to wait another year before the Police had even the glimmering of a hit."

Eventually, the band did come down and played in some pubs in London but the other two members weren't prepared to uproot themselves from Newcastle and they disbanded at the end of February after a gig at the Red Cow in Hammersmith.

Sting at least had the Police to fall back on. Gerry Richardson had no such safety net and was thrown back on his own resources. He did have some success and became musical director for Billy Ocean for a while, but things didn't progress from there and he succumbed to being another casualty of Sting's ambition.

Not that he blames Sting entirely. "I can never feel that angry with Sting for deserting me so to speak. It *was* a close relationship and the split did just about kill me. But he moved down with his wife and baby and he had to jump in any direction where he thought it might happen."

Sting accepts his share of the blame without an apology. "I fucked Gerry up. Not deliberately, but I fucked him up. I was very saddened because I never meant to . . . there's a history of that with me. People get burnt and I'm not that apologetic about it. I know it happens — musically and socially. I've always said that ambition is stronger than friendship and people have been shocked by that but I actually believe it. I'm not justifying it morally; I'm just saying I think that."

But Sting wasn't the complete answer to Stewart's problems. As he says "When Sting came down as far as I was concerned he was joining my band and I didn't have a guitarist for that band. I'd put advertisements in the music papers and I was talking to musicians all over London, but it was depressing. Either it was people who'd have nothing to do with me as soon as I mentioned punk, which meant that there were no musicians I could draw on. Or, on the other hand, there were people who were talking about punk but who had no playing ability . . ."

Henry Padovani was 24.

He was born in Corsica and commuted between there and Algeria where his parents were teachers until the early 60s when he came to mainland France and went to school and then studied Economics at Aix en Provence.

"That's when I started listening to Jimi Hendrix." Like Stewart, the influence was formative and before long he'd got his own band together called Lupus made up of various school friends. The only brief interruption came in 1975 when he was called up for his national service. "They threw me out after three weeks. I was being really naughty. They couldn't stand me.

"I went back to Aix and then the Flaming Groovies came for a concert at the university. They were just too much I talked to them backstage and then I went round to their hotel and spent half the night talking and playing guitar. I was so amazed I decided that night I had to leave."

The Flaming Groovies were heading for London where Henry already had an invitation to stay with Paul Mulligan who he'd met the previous summer and who just happened to be a friend of Stewart Copeland.

So he packed everything he owned into his Renault and drove to London. "The journey was awful. I spent a lot of the time on my own. I was quite shy and I wouldn't talk to people. When I got to London it took me five hours driving around before I found Paul's house."

That was in December 1976. "The first thing I did was to go and see the Flaming Groovies again. I met them all

Stewart: "Every week I'd get a date on Tuesday for that Friday or Saturday and it would be too late for the music papers so I'd haul out the Xerox and run off these handbills . . . and stick them up outside all the other clubs like Dingwalls, the Marquee and the Roxy and . . . nobody would turn up!"

and it was great. Then Paul took me to Curved Air's last gig at St. Albans. It was pretty boring I thought. But I got talking to Stewart afterwards and he said 'You play guitar? Come round and have a blow'.

"I went round and and he had lots of new songs – really frantic ones – and he was writing with his tape recorder. He took me down to the Roxy Club to see the Damned: that was really something He told me 'Henry, this is what's going to happen'. I decided I was going to play for one of these bands. But I felt totally rejected at the Roxy because I had long hair and a beard. I couldn't chat up a girl or anything. I didn't care about my hair very much so I got it cut." That same night, Stewart alleges, Henry also had his first acid trip.

Henry auditioned for a band called London and got offered the job. "But when I told Stewart he went up in the air and started talking about his own band. So I decided to go with him."

Stewart remembers that Henry didn't look much like a punk to start with. "He had long hair and a beard and was very quiet. He'd jammed with a few people but he'd never played in a band before. He couldn't speak much English but he'd picked up some musicians' slang and he used to say 'Where can I put my homp (amplifier)?' or 'where do I put my rope (lead)?'.

"He knew a few chords and he was really enthusiastic and when he'd had his hair cut and stuff he really looked the part. I mean, he could play guitar better than I could and I could play guitar better than Joe Strummer . . . well, in those days

"So I reckoned he'd be OK but I didn't figure Sting would see it that way which is why I gave Henry this

39

Miles Copeland: "Stewart says I wasn't interested in the early days of the band. He forgets that nobody was interested in his group then."

private coaching. He used to come over early before Sting to rehearse or he'd stay on late and I'd teach him the new songs because Sting would have flipped if he'd heard Henry saying 'Now, what fret do I put my finger on for that chord'. So I'd teach him the songs first and then pretend to teach him all over again with Sting. Keeping Sting talking to Henry was a bit of a problem."

Not surprisingly, Sting rumbled Henry's technical deficiencies at once. "Henry was deadweight in that sense. I just couldn't write guitar parts for him because he couldn't play them. He had feel and spirit but for what I wanted he was wrong."

But at least Stewart had a band and before playing any gigs they decided to record a single. They had no chance of getting a major record company interested in them. Most of the people responsible for signing new bands were handling punk in the same way as they would lift a public toilet seat — gingerly and with distaste if they had to. But there were other possibilities.

Miles Copeland was one of the first to see that punk could become its own cottage industry. He'd set up Faulty Products, an independent company which dealt with the business end of punk — managing bands and releasing records on a variety of labels.

Nick Jones, a loyal servant of Miles's who'd stayed with him through the disintegration of BTM, had been watching the birth of punk in the delivery room — the bands and the fanzines. The hottest of these home-made fan magazines was *Sniffin' Glue* whose music lesson was: 'This is a chord, this is another chord, now go and form a band'. Its editor was Mark Perry, his office was his bedroom.

"I was down at the Marquee Club with some members of Climax Blues Band," recalls Nick. "We were talking about *Sniffin' Glue* when Marked poked me in the back and we started chatting. A few weeks later Miles came into the office and there were all these people pasting up pages of *Sniffin' Glue*, using his phone and running up his electricity bill.

"Miles met Mark and said 'Hi, any new bands out there?'. We said 'Sure, come down the Roxy Club tonight'. We took him down to see Generation X and Chelsea. It was the opening night of the Roxy I think."

Miles took the hint: "Punk was like a light bulb going on in my head, an escape from the morass I'd got myself into. People like Stewart, Gene October from Chelsea and Mark Perry were always talking about this or that new group that they'd seen. I'd been used to artists who were jealous — 'screw or be screwed'. But these musicians were asking me to help the other guy. I was floored

"A lot of people said I wasn't honest in what I was doing because one day I was in progressive music and the next I was in punk. Well, I believed in what I was doing *more* than the rest because I had seen the other side. I'd been through the shit of it.

"Sure, when I first saw the Clash I thought it was ridiculous because these guys could hardly play. It took time to adjust my perceptions. But then I got into the excitement of it which is what I'd been missing." While others were moaning about the lack of talent and finesse in punk, Miles saw it for what it was. "Since when has music had anything to do with it? We're in the culture business, the *expression* business."

Expressing himself, Stewart borrowed £150 from Paul Mulligan and booked a recording session at Pathway Studios (where Last Exit had done their demo tapes) for February 12, 1977.

They chose one of Stewart's songs — 'Fall Out'. "We spent one day recording it, that was all," remembers Henry. "It worked quite well and we went home with the tapes really excited — that voice of Sting and us playing fast; it came out sounding a bit like Deep Purple!"

Stewart put on the guitar solo in the middle and Henry played rhythm guitar. The B-side, 'Nothing Achieving', is credited to 'S & I Copeland'. Ian is proud of his role: "Back in the days when we were sharing the apartment Stewart came to me with all these riffs and said 'Have you got any lyrics?' He took some phrases I'd written down, threw out all but a line or two and built up the lyrics from that — and then gave me a credit! It was nice to be able to point it out to people and say 'see that!'."

Now it was time to play some gigs while Stewart was arranging the mixing and pressing of the record and designing the cover. He was hanging around the offices of Faulty Products and latched on to a tour that was being set up for American punk singer Cherry Vanilla.

She hadn't got any record company backing so she could only afford to bring her guitarist with her. But Stewart had an ingenious suggestion: "We'd give her a bass player and drummer — Sting and I — and the equipment, and the Police would go on first and get paid £15 a night. Which meant that we got paid but she sometimes didn't.

"So we did a week's rehearsal with her while Henry was waiting in the wings. And then, just before the first gig at the Newport Stowaway Club in Wales at the beginning of March we had one Police rehearsal. And Henry had forgotten all the chords and stuff. Sting was going 'Oh Jesus *Christ*' because the Cherry Vanilla band was really quite good.

"I was thinking 'Oh no, now my band's going to get stolen by Cherry Vanilla!'. I remember we were putting the gear away at the end of this incredibly awful non-rehearsal in a state of trauma. But we went down and made our debut. It lasted all of forty minutes. We made it; all the way through the set." It was a set made up mostly of Stewart's songs including 'Kids To Blame' which he'd written and recorded with Curved Air plus a couple by Sting.

Stewart also remembers their first London gig at the gritty Nashville Rooms in Kensington. "It was in front of the punk crowd who used to be at every gig — people like Mark Perry, 'the punkometer', and so forth.

"Sting said 'OK, we're a punk band and we're gonna play some punk now. That means the words are banal and the music's fast. So here's a punk song for you, you assholes'. Everyone knew that Sting was being a charlatan I suppose, but he was perfectly frank about it. Miles didn't approve of him at that time and when Miles doesn't like someone he just ignores them. In those early days Sting still sounded pretty jazzy, bending notes and so forth."

It's no exaggeration to say that the Police were *nobody's* idea of a punk band. Stewart's former identity with Curved Air was held up to support charges of bandwagon jumping and before long Sting's jazz-rock past was uncovered for similar ridicule.

"That first band was pretty rough," remembers Nick Jones. "In all honesty I can't say a Police gig was high on the agenda of the *Sniffin' Glue* scene. Mark Perry *had* to put them down. He was an honest guy. Just because he was receiving help and encouragement from Stewart's elder brother he wouldn't endorse something he didn't believe in. I'm sure Miles would have thought more of them if Mark had said it was good but it couldn't be done."

Later in March the Police hitched a ride with another American punk outfit, Wayne County And The Electric Chairs, for a tour of Holland and a concert in Paris at the Palais de Glace. Again, Stewart's experience in rock 'n' roll diplomacy paid dividends. "It was the first big punk event in Paris. There was Generation X, the Jam, Wayne County and us, the pariahs of the London scene.

"When we arrived Generation X and the Jam were bitching about who should go on before us. We had to go on immediately before Wayne County because we were using their equipment. But their equipment hadn't turned up so I stepped in quick and did a deal with Generation X that they could go on last and close the show if we could use their equipment. And Generation X bought it.

"So the Jam came on and did really well. We came on and did so-so. Wayne County And The Electric Chairs were fantastic and while Generation X were setting themselves up and arguing and generally being total idiots the kids all went home!"

Henry thought the band got better during their European tour: "At times we would play better than Wayne and we would feel that we were getting there and that would pull us together. Sting put in a new song called 'Don't Give Up Your Daytime Job' (the old Last Exit number) around then and I remember we attracted some attention from a Dutch record company. But we went back to England and it was ... the same old routine I suppose."

In April they played another series of gigs across England with Cherry Vanilla and at the beginning of May 'Fall Out' was released on Illegal Records, a label formed by Stewart for the purpose. Stewart had handled every aspect of the record's release, from designing the cover and putting the record in the sleeve to selling it to the shops.

"We sold 10,000 copies in all, mainly through the big distributors who'd take 250 at a time obviously. But it took a lot of time, on top of everything else I was supposed to do, like getting gigs, keeping the band together and rehearsing. I went into the office every day and in between the usual calls I'd have to get out the telephone book and find a list of record shops and phone them. I'd pick an area, find a town and look up a likely store and ring them and introduce myself and try to sell the record.

"Meanwhile on the next desk there was Miles' salesgirl saying 'Yes, we have the new Chelsea single and Sham 69 and the Fall' and I'd be whispering across 'And who else have you got?' while she was talking on the phone.

"Miles wasn't giving us the elbow, he just wasn't giving us the time of day: two different things! He would say 'Why don't you come over here and do this for me?', or 'Have you thought about joining the John Cale band?'.

"He was morally helpful and he let me use his office as well as Pete Mannheim from the booking agency who used to get us all our early gigs. He couldn't book us for love or money but we used to step in when there was a cancellation. So all our gigs were advertized as someone else!

"Every week I'd get a date on Tuesday for that Friday or Saturday and it would be too late for the music papers so I'd haul out the Xerox and run off these handbills saying 'The Police at the Hope and Anchor' or wherever and go and stick them outside all the other clubs like Dingwalls, the Marquee and the Roxy and ... nobody would turn up! For our audience we could count on three girlfriends and maybe about ten other people."

Miles remains unapologetic about his lack of involvement: "Stewart says I wasn't interested in the early days of the band. He forgets that nobody was interested in his group then. Any time Caroline Coon or Mark Perry made a comment about them it was 'The Police – yawn'."

Sting's commitment to that first band was also shaky to say the least: "During the first six months of the Police I didn't take it seriously at all ... Being in the band was just a big joke, but by dint of Stewart's entrepreneurial abilities and his enthusiasm we actually made some money. We made £15 a night with Cherry Vanilla which was a coup. Stewart is an incredible person! But that whole thing ... I was appalled. I went along with it like playing in a cabaret. It was dire.

"I infiltrated a few songs at the beginning – 'Visions Of The Night', 'Don't Give Up Your Daytime Job', 'Landlord' and 'Dead End Job' which I wrote the words for. It's still my favorite Police song. It's totally irrelevant now but at the time there was a lot of real angst; real 'fuck you', which I like. It's funny too. I love it."

Stewart remembers another Sting song which had its title changed drastically to fit the fashion: "Sting had this song called 'Love Is In My Heart' I think. He'd been down in London for a couple of months and he'd gone to the Roxy and the Vortex and he was still writing songs about his heart! The first time we played it I was making out the set list and I asked him what it was called. When I heard I went 'whaaat?'. I changed it to 'Three O'Clock Shit' for the sake of the set list!" Sting gruffly puts the story down to Stewart's imagination.

But Sting wasn't the only one who was dissatisfied. To Henry, the band he'd joined didn't match the ideals that he and his friends were finding in the punk movement. "I was becoming part of this whole scene. And it was my *first* scene remember? Not like Stewart and Sting. I didn't worry that there was no money because I was new – even newer than the rest of the kids in the sense that I'd only been in London a few months. Stewart and Sting were used to having some money before so they'd try and make it through the week and not go out. I can understand it now but I didn't care at all then, they really bored me in that way.

"I had a lot of new friends by then. We would go out to the clubs and go bananas. After that it would be sobering to go back to Stewart and Sting. I wasn't compromising ... I was here to do my thing."

Stewart's band was hanging together by a thread. Nobody had an encouraging word. His own commitment, both to punk and the Police, was never in doubt though. Nick Jones is emphatic: "I'm sure Stewart was as excited by punk as we all were at Faulty. He understood the energy and encompassed its spirit.

"He was a classic case of a skilled musician unlearning

everything again — one of those people whose peer group was saying 'it will never happen' when in the London clubs it *was* all happening."

Stewart agrees: "All my friends from Caravan, Climax Blues Band and everybody in Curved Air apart from Sonja thought I was socially unacceptable." But he refutes any suggestion that he was playing down his talents in any way with the Police: "I think I was able to use more of my talent with the Police than I was with Curved Air. In Curved Air I had to keep laying back. With the Police I went berserk; I played like a madman."

He also stresses that the only differences he had with Henry were over his playing ability: "He was an enthusiastic, helpful and useful member of the group in every other way. He and I went out and painted the city — our graffiti are still up around London and I still get a kick every time I drive past them."

Despite accusations that Stewart was an imposter, he knew exactly where he stood: "I remember saying to Sting at the beginning 'Don't let's go for chart hits which don't really mean anything. Let's go for one group of people and really hit them hard. Let's put everything into one objective — sound — and then we can get a small following which is dedicated rather than a following which is dependent on whether or not we get airplay and will leave us if we don't.

"Looking at it from our own point of view, we had to select somebody to aim at. At the beginning we selected 'The Punks' — that's our connection. It's not the music we wanted to play but it was the people we wanted to focus in on."

As the Police stagnated, Stewart had his work cut out trying to hang on to Sting. Gerry Richardson had already tried to recruit him for Billy Ocean's backing band when he'd become the musical director and had offered him £90 a week which must have been tempting.

And Stewart knew that Sting's commitment was less than wholehearted: "He didn't identify with the group. His attitude was 'Convince me — keep me in the band'.

"So every day I'd phone him up and I'd always have something to tell him. Like 'I've just got the photos back from the session', or 'I've just finished the record sleeve, why don't you come over and have a look at it', or 'We've got a gig'. I always tried to have something happening. Whereas with all the other scenes there wasn't much going on. It was 'Oh . . . I'll call you next week', or 'Maybe, if the record company comes up with the money'."

But he must have realized that Sting and Henry were irreconcilable. One of them would have to go and unless he could find a replacement for Henry then it would be Sting. And the longer this uneasy truce lasted the more chance there was of somebody filching Sting from under Stewart's nose.

So when Mike Howlett, a former bass player with Gong who knew Sting through Virgin Publishing, asked Sting to join him in a band called Strontium 90 which was going to play a one-off gig at a Gong reunion in Paris, Stewart had every reason to be suspicious.

His suspicions were not allayed when Mike roped him in as the drummer for the group. But Mike didn't need Henry. He had another guitarist called Andy Summers . . .

4
ANDY: HAVE YOU MET MY GUITARIST?

"I don't go along with the myth that you're supposed to have more credibility if you come from the working-class because it gives you something to kick against. These days I think coming from the bourgoisie is a much harder thing to get away from — it's much more insidious."

If Andy Summers' childhood lacks either the glamorous elements of Stewart's upbringing or the working-class chip on the shoulder that characterizes Sting, he has at least shown the ability to rise above the largest and most amorphous section of the British population — the middle-class.

"I never had a tremendous need to escape some kind of grimy background," he says. "I think that's a little clichéd and tends to be couched in romantic terms that don't always justify what you get at the end. I had a pretty decent childhood. I can't say it was fraught with trauma."

Andrew James Summers was born in Poulton-le-Fylde near Blackpool on December 31, 1942. He was a wartime baby and his father was in the RAF but when he was 2 the family moved south to Bournemouth where his father ran a restaurant. He had an elder brother Tony, a younger brother Richard and a sister Monica.

He spent his childhood cushioned to some extent against the grey aftermath of the war — ration books and demob suits. Bournemouth is a large but genteel seaside town on the south coast, unscathed by the ravages of the industrial revolution that blight the northern half of the country.

Apart from having piano lessons, Andy can recall no details of his early years before his teens. "At about 14 or 15 I would go round with my friends feeling totally alienated from people. We'd be sneering and laughing at everyone we came across because we felt so different. From that time on I just wanted to get away from Bournemouth and up to London where there was something happening.

"I always had a bent for music. I was interested in it at school and I started listening to jazz before I ever had any instruments. My older brother was a fanatic. He had a large collection of records and used to play a lot of Charlie Parker, Stan Kenton and people like that. I was given a guitar when I was 14 and it turned into an overnight obsession which has lasted ever since.

"Someone turned up at the house with this guitar. It apparently belonged to an uncle of mine. I started by playing the songs of the day. A number of kids at school had got guitars too so I tried learning from them. It was really the only thing I was interested in.

"I left school after taking O-levels and went to work in a music shop, but I couldn't stand it. At that time the big event in my life was every Friday when there was a modern jazz club called the Blue Note in town and the musicians who played there were really good. Eventually they let me play in the interval."

Which is where he first met George 'Zoot' Money, a window cleaner, extrovert character and keyboard player of local renown. "I used to sing traditional jazz even though I was essentially a rocker," says Zoot. "I used to hang around with some pretty greasy types.

"Andy stood out as being a class guitarist even then. He interested me because he could commit music to memory and reproduce it when he needed to. He could copy just about anything. He was 16 at the time but he looked nearer 12. He's always looked much younger than he was and at that time he was quite sensitive about it."

Andy's spot at the Blue Note started as a joke. A common feature of the jazz record scene were recordings of bands billed as 'The So-And-So All Stars' because the various members were contracted to different record labels. So Andy, who would turn up each week with a different bunch of musicians, would be introduced as 'The Andy Summers All Stars'.

"This whole legend grew up around me," recalls Andy. "Obviously I was knocked out by it all. They'd make other announcements like 'There will be a meeting of the Andy Summers Fan Club in the telephone kiosk across the road after the show'. But finally I got good enough to play with the main band."

His parents didn't discourage him: "I think my mother realized that I meant it. I stopped working in the shop and began playing a residency at a hotel three or four nights a week. So I was making more money than I had been before."

Bournemouth has always had a thriving local music

scene and has produced its fair share of distinctive British rock musicians such as Greg Lake (Emerson Lake and Palmer), John Wetton (King Crimson, Roxy Music, Uriah Heep and UK) and Al Stewart. And when Andy left his residency at the hotel he handed over to another young guitarist called Robert Fripp who went on to form King Crimson.

When these musicians weren't playing professionally they'd all meet up at the Downstairs Club in the town. "We'd all go and collect our unemployment benefit together and jam at this club over the weekend," says Andy.

It was 1963 and the British rock scene was just experiencing the first tremors of the Beat Boom upheaval that was to catapult it from an underground obscurity to a dominant force in the space of a year. In Bournemouth the problem was not apathy but the lack of any properly formed bands who could take advantage of it and grab a piece of the action.

Someone was going to have to make the break on their own. And it was Zoot who did it: "I got an offer to join Alexis Korner's Blues Incorporated which was a great opportunity so I went straight up to London and started playing with him."

Korner can fairly claim to be the godfather of the British Beat although he'd probably agree to share the title with John Mayall. He gave a start to such names as Mick Jagger, Keith Richard, Charlie Watts, Robert Plant, Jack Bruce and Eric Burdon.

Being an eager youth, Zoot asked Alexis if he might play a short set of his own between the band's two shows. Alexis agreed and Zoot got Andy and drummer Colin Allen to come up and help him out.

A few weeks later a manager/promoter called Bob Hind came up to Zoot after a gig and asked if he fancied playing with his own band full-time. The market for Zoot's black R&B was expanding and the Flamingo Club in Soho needed to replace Georgie Fame who was moving on to bigger things. And so the Zoot Money Big Roll Band was formed with the nucleus of Zoot, Andy (who 'commemorated' his move from home by changing his name from Summers to Somers for the next few years), Colin Allen and Nick Newall on saxophone. The line-up fluctuated but was generally a six-piece.

"We were living together in a bedsit in Finchley," recalls Andy. "In fact we were even sleeping together in the same bed! The first night we appeared at the Flamingo there were lots of black GIs down there and they thought we were great because we played lots of R&B like Ray Charles, Jimmy McGriff, James Brown and Jimmy Smith – Zoot's Hammond organ was ideal for all that.

"The club manager Rik Gunnell asked us to play regularly. He also had this agency and so we started playing the circuit. It was a good time to be in London with the Beatles and the Stones just starting to make an impact.

"Some weeks we actually managed to play 13 gigs – it was unbelievable. We'd go out of town to somewhere like the Ricky Tick at Windsor on Friday and come back for an all-nighter at the Flamingo. On Saturday it might be Hounslow before another all-nighter at the Flamingo and we'd get home about eight on Sunday morning. We'd wake up at one o' clock and drive to Douglas House which was the American air base in London. In the evening we'd play somewhere like the Black Prince in Bexley and then come back for another all-nighter. We'd carry all our own gear and play two sets everywhere we went. People don't seem to work like that any more!

"We had to be really tight musically and put on a good show. We worked ourselves up to £400 a night which was a lot of dough in those days." Zoot could always be relied upon to provide outrageous visual antics such as the trouser-dropping escapades seen by Sting in Newcastle.

Andy was the group member who most closely resembled the archetypal 60s pop star, Zoot recalls: "He always looked neat. It was good for pulling the birds and I used to use him as bait – 'Have you met my guitarist?'. If there were two girls Andy would get the better looking one and I'd be left with the other. I didn't mind because mine was usually a safer bet!"

But record successes always eluded the Big Band, perhaps because they didn't resemble the typical beat group. The closest they got was a single called 'Big Time Operator' in the summer of 1966 which reached the Top Thirty.

By the spring of 1967 the R&B boom had started to run itself into the ground and there were the first inklings

Andy with Kevin Coyne (the only other beardless one).

Zoot Money's Big Roll Band: "Some weeks we actually managed to play 13 gigs."

of another musical trait that was to take over and dominate the scene for the next three or four years — psychedelia.

"The whole atmosphere was changing," remembers Andy. "By now Zoot and I were living in this house in West Kensington. Zoot's place became the scene for many a wild party where people like Paul McCartney, Jimi Hendrix, the Moody Blues and so on would end up after going to clubs like Blaises or the Cromwellian.

"We were also very good friends with the Animals and they would come back from American tours talking about 'taking trips'. At first I didn't know what they meant by it."

Like Stewart, Andy isn't keen to recommend LSD to anyone now. But it's impossible to discuss the musical developments of the late 60s without talking about drugs, and particularly LSD, because of the crucial role they played. "My life altered," says Andy simply.

"Hilton Valentine of the Animals gave me my first trip. I had no idea what to expect. He gave me this tab and after about 45 minutes I thought nothing was happening. Then Hilton said 'I think you're about ready now', and he started reading from Timothy Leary's book *The Psychedelic Experience*. It begins something like 'Oh voyager, you are about to enter the nameless journey' and I was thinking 'Oh yeah?'.

"Suddenly his face began to change in front of me until it was in vivid technicolor. I thought 'someone's playing a trick on me'. Then the floor texture started changing and the whole trip began. I was a virgin mind and the first acid trip is the best one ever. My first few acid trips were all deeply religious experiences and I started to get the White Light and all that. It sounds a bit silly talking about it now, but that was the era.

"There was something else that happened that day. I'd been living with this girl for about two years on and off. I was pretty young and she was a very wilful girl. She was having this scene with Eric Burdon as well. She'd been in hospital having an abortion. I think it was my child but it was a bit difficult to tell. But that day I was supposed to bring her home. So in the midst of all this I got to the hospital and she'd gone. I was so hurt; she'd gone off with Eric. Later on that night I'm back home still freaking out when she walks in with Eric. And I've got this big issue to deal with while I'm on acid. Eventually we just floated over the whole thing."

The effect of LSD on the Big Roll Band was to transform them into a psychedelic four-piece called Dantalions Chariot with Zoot, Andy and Colin plus new bassist Pat Donaldson. "Conceptually the two bands were the same," explains Zoot. "We were just trying to stay with what was happening."

The group was quickly adopted by the burgeoning London underground scene who would gather every Friday night at a basement club in Tottenham Court Road called the Blarney which they christened UFO. "We were the first band in the country to use two overhead oil machines at every gig, even before the Pink Floyd," says Zoot. These machines projected multicolored moving amoeba-like shapes. "We also had two variable pulse strobe lights which were independently controlled. You're not allowed to do that now because it can induce epilepsy. All our clothes and gear were white so that the oil machines could take over."

They signed to CBS and released a single called 'Madman Running Through The Fields' which was a cult hit. But outside the circle of flower children nobody could really understand what was going on. "People just weren't ready for it," says Andy. "In those days they wanted to hear hits.

"I remember walking into the Marquee one night and the manager was standing in the corridor holding his ears. I asked if I could come in and he said 'You don't have to pay, if you can stand that noise you're welcome'. And there were the Pink Floyd and this great sheet of sound – it was fantastic."

This section of Andy's career is documented in a book called *Groupie* written by Jenny Fabian, which is a no-holds barred account of her social life with only the names changed to protect the not-so innocent. Andy has a cameo role (roll?) early in the book and he freely admits that as far as his contribution is concerned, nothing is exaggerated: "She remembered all the conversations we had. I wrote her a note when I came back from America and she put it in the book word for word. There's nothing in there to be ashamed of." But then a man whose genitals are described as 'perfectly formed' is unlikely to have too many complaints.

Dantalions Chariot only lasted a year. "The truth was we were doing very badly outside London and Zoot was starting to get paranoid about things. He thought he was throwing away his career," says Andy.

"We also had this serious car crash which really finished the group. We were driving across the Yorkshire Moors in the middle of the night and the car went off the road at about 50 miles per hour and turned over three times. I couldn't stand up when I got out. The only thing I'd broken was my nose but my back was so badly bruised it took me about a year to get over it."

Colin Allen went on to join Stone The Crows and Focus, Pat Donaldson joined Fairport Convention and Joan Armatrading and Zoot joined the Animals in America. And Andy had already paved the way to join Soft Machine, one of the more avant-garde bands to emerge out of the psychedelic movement.

"I'd become good friends with Robert Wyatt the drummer, and I could see that Dantalions Chariot's days were numbered. I went to live with Robert down in Dulwich and got involved with the 'Canterbury set' – all the people in Caravan and Soft Machine who'd come out of the Wild Flowers.

This was in the spring of 1968 and Soft Machine had just completed one traumatic and debauched tour of America with Jimi Hendrix and were girding their loins and minds for another.

"Basically I joined a sinking ship. I liked the music but the tour was truly awful. We'd do a sixty minute set with no breaks – just a continuous sound and monotonous chants like 'We Did It Again'. People used to freak! But we paved the way for a lot of things that came after that.

"When we got back to New York after the tour we were really miserable. Kevin Ayers only wanted to tour with the Soft Machine as a trio so I left the group." In the space of four months Andy had seen two groups collapse around him. "I was a bit depressed but I thought 'Well, here I am in America. I'm damned if I'm going to go back now'.

"So I stayed on at the Chelsea Hotel. I called up Zoot in Los Angeles and they were just getting rid of one of their guitarists so there was a slot available. I went straight out and joined them. It was perfect."

Andy shared the guitar role with John Weider, alternating on bass guitar. "It worked out all right but Andy was never keen on bands with two guitarists," says Zoot. "I remember meeting him shortly after he'd joined the Police while it was still a four-piece. I could see what was going to happen..."

Only Eric Burdon remained from the original Animals but they'd had big hits with 'San Franciscan Nights' and 'Monterey'. "Suddenly I was out in California and a member of a world famous group," says Andy. "I was living with Eric in Laurel Canyon and into a whole new scene. I did think it was a bit of a downward step musically but what happened was that Zoot and I took over the group. We just started carrying on as if it was Dantalions Chariot." On the next Animals' album, 'Love Is', they even recorded a new version of 'Madam Running Through The Fields'.

"My first gig with them was at the Newport Pop Festival in front of 100,000 people and we stole the show! We blew off Jefferson Airplane and the Grateful Dead. But the problem was that the band got too good for Eric on stage and he started to get insecure about it, so we sowed the seeds of our own destruction."

One incident that speeded up the Animals demise was the celebrated 'Japanese affair'. "We were supposed to go to Japan in September 1968 but we didn't actually get there until November by the time we'd obtained the visas. We meant to be there for three weeks and play a dozen concerts but when we got there we found there was a gig every day. The contract hadn't been honored at all. We were supposed to be paid in cash before each gig but they were only giving us half.

Zoot Money (probably).

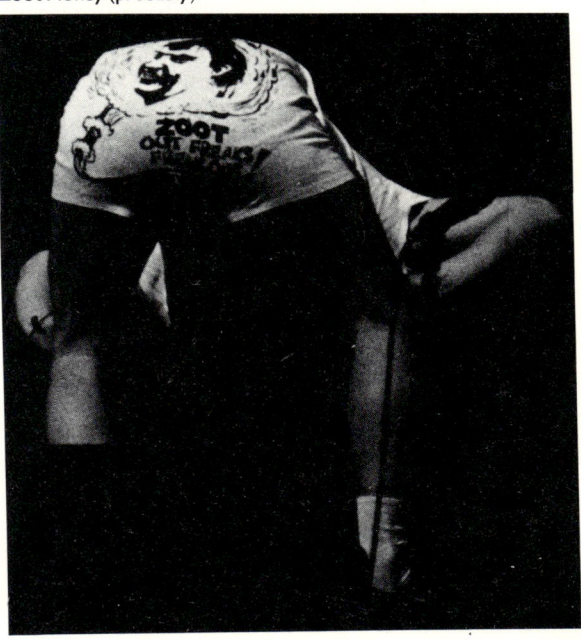

"We ended up playing in a small club and we couldn't fathom why because we were supposed to be a big deal in Japan. It turned out we were working for the Japanese mafia and while we were on stage they kidnaped our manager. They held him in a room and demanded that he write an IOU for 25,000 dollars. They said they'd lost money because we hadn't turned up in September. They held a gun at his head and were threatening to cut off a finger. Finally they escorted him back to the hotel and told him that if we didn't all leave the next day we would be killed.

"We knew nothing about all this. When we finished the show the others went back to the hotel and I went off with this Californian girl I'd met. I got back to the hotel the next morning and there was no one there until one of the roadies turned up looking pale. He related the entire story to me and took me out to the airport where they were sitting in a sheepish little bundle waiting for the plane. We lost all our equipment and I think that was probably the final nail in the coffin for Eric."

The Animals broke up at the end of 1968 which meant that Andy was out of work again and broke. "I never got any royalties. It was terrible. But it taught me a lesson. It never happened again."

He returned to England briefly before recording a solo album in California, playing everything except drums. It was never released but Al Clark, an executive at Virgin Records, remembers hearing a tape of it. "It was full of the quirks of the time. The songs definitely reflected his Californian location."

Andy's fortunes were drifting downwards: "The manager of the Animals was supposed to be getting me a record deal but he got arrested on a rape charge and fled the country. That was the end of that. I was finished – down to my last five dollars."

He went to live with a girlfriend called Robin Lane, Neil Young's 'Cinnamon Girl', who emerged in 1980 with her own band, Robin Lane And The Chartbusters. She took care of him and they married. Andy stopped playing guitar and for a while drifted into acting in Hollywood theater groups.

"Then I started playing classical guitar and another whole area of music opened up." Then he enrolled at San Fernando State College where he studied for the next three and a half years. "I was totally immersed in classical music. I was studying harmony, counterpoint and conducting.

"Financially I was hanging on by a thread. I was surviving by giving guitar lessons and I was living on about 15 dollars a week. California's about the only place where you can do that in America. I just studied and practised classical guitar for about ten hours a day. I wasn't listening to rock 'n' roll at all. I even had designs on becoming a concert guitarist.

"Eventually I decided that, much as I loved it, it wasn't going to be exactly what I wanted out of life. I suddenly got very depressed. My marriage started to fall apart and it got to a period when I couldn't even get out of bed in the morning. I just couldn't see any point in it."

This was the lowest point in Andy's life. Total tail spin. To pull out of it, he turned to his original obsession. "Rock 'n' roll was about the only thing I could do. I hadn't played an electric guitar for three years but I went out and bought one.

"I got a job with a Mexican band for a couple of months down in east Los Angeles, playing to Mexican audiences. I was gradually getting back into it. Parts of it were painful – the process of getting back into the rock 'n' roll world again – but I did it.

"When I'd stopped playing and living in a world which was going round from gig to gig it was a shock to me – living a normal life and seeing how people really lived. Because rock 'n' roll is such a hermetically sealed world."

Having moved away from Robin he shared a house with Paul Michael Glaser (Starsky from the TV cop series). He also toyed with acting again but an introduction to Tim Rose put him firmly back on the track.

Rose – an American singer/songwriter who'd had a couple of classic hits in the 60s with 'Morning Dew' and 'Come Away Melinda', was also trying to pick up the pieces and together they formed a band, and started to play gigs.

"Tim was a real Anglophile and I wanted to come back after five and a half years away. We'd made some tapes and we decided to try and get a record deal together in England."

After five years away from rock 'n' roll Andy had revised his perspectives for his return: "I'd been through my youth in a kind of unconscious haze and I felt that I'd arrived at last. I'd been through a lot – I'd done all the drugs, and had a really colorful life. I'd watched musicians drop away left right and center – the carnage was dreadful – but I was young enough and fit enough. And I could play, and I had the ego that wanted to succeed. The need to be an artist and a supreme musician was the strongest force.

"I came back to England very deliberately to have a career. I was always aware of trying to make moves forward to gain a better position for myself and get more out of it."

He arrived back in November 1973 with his new girlfriend Kate who he married soon afterwards. "I was intending to scrape around until something happened. Tim was going to come over later so I got a flat in Shepherds Bush and started letting people know I was back.

"I'd got down to my last few pounds before I met Robert Fripp at the Speakeasy. He put me in touch with Mike Giles who'd been the drummer in King Crimson. In fact I'd been in the Boy Scouts with him! He was about to go on tour with Neil Sedaka and said he might be able to get me in.

"That same night Sedaka's wife called me and asked if I was interested. But I couldn't afford to buy an amplifier so I had to go to Neil and ask him to lend me £300 so I could buy one. It was a real nerve but he lent me the money. He'd never even heard me play!"

Andy toured with Neil until the summer of 1974 and recorded an album with him called 'Live At The Festival Hall'. "That was my first gig with him. I was thrown in at the deep end. You can't really hear much of me because it was recorded with the Royal Philharmonic Orchestra."

For the rest of that summer Andy played sessions and recorded an album with Tim Rose who'd finally come over called 'The Singer' but the projected band failed to materialize. In the autumn he landed a six-week tour with David Essex, the latest teenybopper hero, and watched the mobbing scenes around the country with wry amusement and not a twinge of déjà-vu.

What Andy needed, though, was a permanent band where he could make a positive contribution. At the beginning of 1975 he got the chance when he joined Kevin Coyne who was just emerging from the club circuit. It was as a result of his growing network of contacts.

The new band went straight into the studio and recorded an album called 'Matching Head And Feet' which was acclaimed by the critics. But Kevin was so concerned with deflating the rock 'n' roll myths that he was unlikely to make a major breakthrough, although Andy remains in awe of his talent.

"Kevin was magnificent on stage. His main prop was a chair and he'd do almost anything you could imagine with it. Sometimes he'd just walk around with it on his head. And he's probably the best lyricist we've got in this country. He's a real genius. It was a bit like working with an unexploded bomb."

After they'd recorded the album a couple of the band left and Andy was able to repay some of Zoot's favors by getting him in. They toured England and Europe incessantly over the next eighteen months or so and Andy locked into life on the road once more, "I never knew him to have a sloppy night with Kevin," recalls Al Clark who was in charge of the band's publicity for Virgin Records. "He was always attentive to what he was doing. He applied the same standards to himself that he applied to his music — he dotted his i's and crossed his t's. He would join in the fun after gigs but always with restraint. He was shrewd as well as sound — it wasn't so much the pursuit of excellence as the pursuit of survival.

"He was always interested in achieving something on his own too. He brought in a single to Virigin to see if we'd be interested in releasing it — it was a version of Santo And Johnny's 'Sleepwalk' (an instrumental hit in the late 50s) with a song he'd written on the B-side." The single was never released as Andy never signed the publishing contract that Virgin wanted as well as the record deal (and in view of Sting's later hassles with Virgin Publishing perhaps it was a blessing in disguise).

The music was good, the wages were good, but in reality Andy's 'progress' had only brought him back to square one — where he'd got to with the Animals seven years earlier. He was a respected session man; he was on a treadmill: "I felt on my own, different. Now I had ambition. I was always looking beyond."

He'd try almost anything. In autumn 1975 he impersonated Mike Oldfield — who was at that time a reclusive character — in an orchestrated version of 'Tubular Bells' at Newcastle City Hall. Supporting them were a jazz-rock combo called Last Exit.

"I know Sting insists he blew us off stage but I watched Last Exit for about three minutes and thought they were lousy. I enjoyed playing 'Tubular Bells' though. The orchestra was a bit diabolical but I was really good!"

Andy linked up with the concert's conductor David Bedford a few months later when he recorded a track for Bedford's new album 'The Odyssey' playing a solo on a track called 'Circe's Island'. He remembers the session well: "David was teaching at Queens College School in London and he got the girls' choir to sing on the album. When I did my solo there were about 15 beautiful schoolgirls in the studio as well. It was inspirational!"

"Andy was never keen on bands with two guitarists. I remember watching him shortly after he'd joined the Police while it was still a four-piece. I could see what was going to happen..." Zoot Money.

Another neo-classical adventure was an album called 'Sarabande' he recorded in Munich with Jon Lord, former Deep Purple keyboard player. It was during those sessions that he met Eberhard Schoener, an avant-garde composer who was to be something of a financial saving grace a year or so later for the Police.

Kevin Coyne's band broke up early in 1976. They'd recorded another studio album called 'Heartburn' and a live album 'In Living Black And White'. But the group just wasn't viable as far as the record company was concerned and Kevin over-reacted to a particularly grueling tour of Europe.

Soon afterwards Andy and Zoot transferred their allegiance to Kevin Ayers. Andy hadn't run across him since their Soft Machine tour in 1968 and Ayers' career had fluctuated since but an album called 'Yes We Have No Mananas — So Get Your Mananas Today' had revived his standing and he formed a new band to take advantage of it.

Andy stayed about a year, touring Europe and in between recording two albums with Eberhard Schoener who had maintained contact with him. At the end of 1976 his musical dodgem car bumped into Mike Howlett.

"I met him at a Christmas party and went over to his house a couple of times. A few months later he asked me to play in Strontium 90 for this concert in Paris. He'd talked about Sting to me a couple of times but I'd never met him."

One day in early May, Andy met up with Mike, Sting and Stewart at the Virtual Earth Studios in Swiss Cottage to rehearse...

49

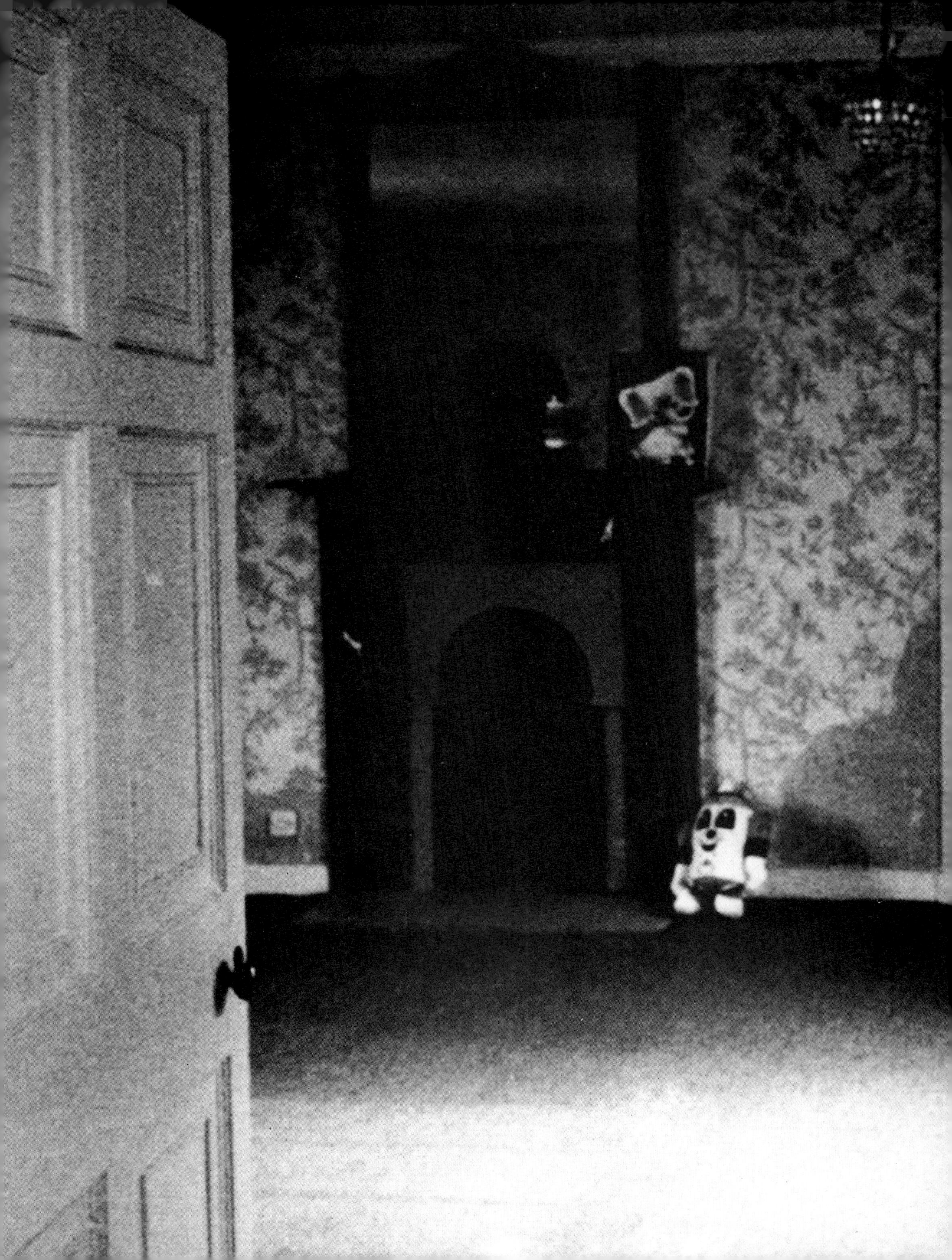

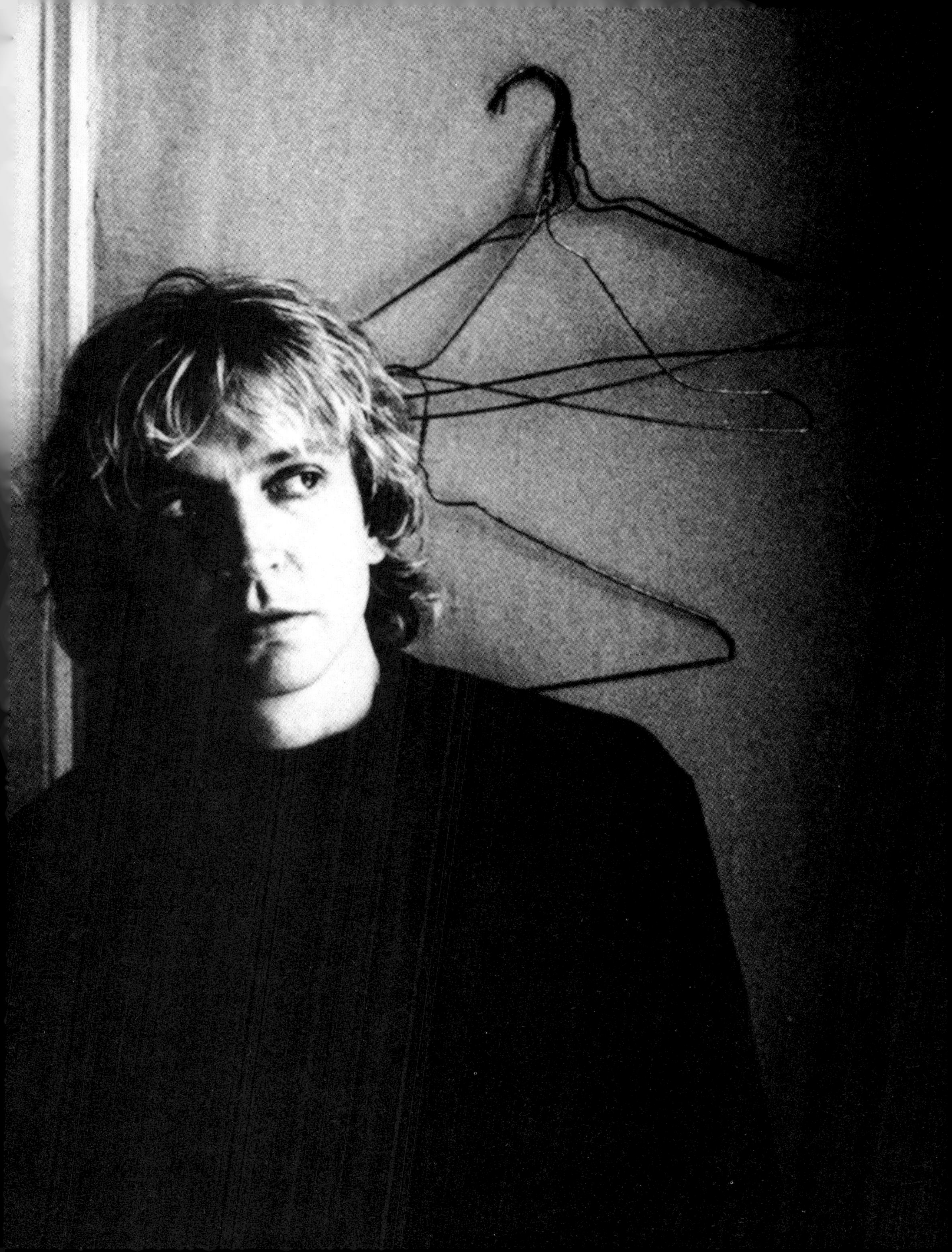

5
THERE'S JUST ONE THING, YOU HAVE TO BE BLOND

"Even while we were rehearsing with Strontium 90, Stewart was thinking of nothing but the Police," says Andy. "It was difficult to be with him; you couldn't really have a conversation with him. It was a dedication, an absolutely fanatical drive."

Stewart agrees: "Mike Howlett was competition. He wanted to steal my group so I stole his group!" For Sting, Strontium 90 did offer an attractive alternative to the creative frustration he'd been feeling with the Police: "Mike was a real musician. Through him we met Andy and there was a chance to play music that was more sophisticated and attuned to what I wanted. But finally I saw a greater possibility in the Police without Mike. I'm not slagging him off, but for the vision we had he was wrong."

Strontium 90 traveled to Paris at the end of May 1977 for the Gong reunion concert which was held in a circus tent in front of 5,000 French hippy fans. "Hey, it's the real brown rice scene man, far out!" was Stewart's comment on seeing the audience. The Strontium 90 line-up — a four-piece with two bass guitarists — was unusual but, as Sting says, "a pretty potent force". The set even included two Police songs, 'Dead End Job' and 'Be My Girl'. At the end Mike told the hippies "C'est autre chose huh? Ça bouge."

The group did play another gig, in London at the Nashville, although they changed their name to the Elevators. But the assembled record company scouts were already preoccupied with punk and Mike's chance to pinch the Police had gone. Sting did leave him a small vinyl legacy, a single called 'Nuclear Waste' recorded for the anti-nuclear campaign with Howlett on bass and Sting on vocals. "They tried to get Johnny Rotten to sing it, but he wouldn't so I did," says Sting.

Andy went back to Kevin Ayers and the Police resumed their uneasy alliance. "We landed our first headline gig," crows Stewart. The Putney Railway Hotel no less.

A few weeks later Andy came down to see them at the Marquee and joined in the encore. He saw right through the group's punk facade: "I thought 'This is phoney'. The suit didn't fit. But at the same time Sting was larger than life and Stewart was a good drummer, there was no question about that. Sting was able to talk to the audience. He could sing and play bass. I could see the potential in them, but it just wasn't being realized."

After Andy's brief intervention Stewart heard Sting muttering: "I'd forgotten the guitar had six strings and there's more than three chords you can play on it." The ground was prepared. It was Andy who made the next move: "I phoned Sting one morning soon afterwards and said 'It seems to me that I should join the group because the three of us could be really strong'. I talked to Sting first because I knew he was getting fed up with the way things were. He sort of agreed.

"After I'd spoken to Sting I went down to Oxford Street and as I got off the tube Stewart got off too. I said hello and asked him to come and have a cup of coffee. I proposed the same thing to him."

Stewart recollects more than a proposal: "Andy pulled me into the café and said 'You guys have a great group except that you need to sack the rhythm guitarist and get a new one — me'. He went into all these arguments about how Henry just wasn't good enough and we weren't being fair to each other. It was almost as if he was already a member of the group and he was giving me a lecture about being late for the bus.

"I said 'We haven't got anything going for us. The record company is me!' I also knew he was quite a meticulous guy — 'Don't breath over my guitar' and that kind of stuff — so I said 'Andy, I know the group would be a lot better if you were in it, but if you did join us the group would break up within a month because you wouldn't be able to handle humping your own equipment into gig after gig'.

"Eventually I told him that Sting's feet were really bad. I was starting to say anything because I just didn't believe him. I just didn't believe he was prepared to chuck in the salary he was getting from Kevin Ayers. The next thing, he calls up Kevin Ayers' management and cancels his weekly retainer!" Stewart adds in some awe: "Andy didn't even need to have done that. He could have kept his retainer and still played with us."

For Andy, who had spent the past four years building up a reputation as a virtuoso guitarist, joining the Police was going to wreck his credibility: "I could have gone on

Islington Hope and Anchor pub, London 1978.

forever being a good side man, but it didn't really suit my character. I wanted more ... more out of it than that. Being in the Police meant I could finally live out a lot of things I would have liked to have done for years. I'd been dealing with session-musician minds and bands and I always felt a sense of frustration with it. And what would have happened to the group if I hadn't joined? I think Sting would have left pretty soon. He was really chafing at the bit. So as far as I'm concerned the Police didn't really start until I joined."

Andy laid down only one condition: that the Police remain a trio. This wasn't going to be easy because both Sting and Stewart felt a loyalty to Henry.

For Sting there was no alternative. He was also aware of the implication: "It was the end of Stewart's band and the only thing that connected us was the name. Stewart was chary about giving up Henry because he was bonafide. But to me it meant giving up the charade. It *was* a pretence and Stewart never actually admitted that to himself. He hung on to that desire for hipness. He still has it. Even now when it's impossible for us to be hip, when we're almost Rod Stewarts. He's the opposite of me in that respect. He was always saying 'Why aren't we like the Clash? Why aren't we like the Damned?' which really annoyed me because I knew we had ten times the music in us. That's why I was ultimately for sacking Henry. To Stewart, without Henry the hipness had gone and we were ... naked,"

Stewart sums up: "Andy bulldozed his way into the group – to the benefit of the group. And the credit that I deserve is that I allowed him to fast-talk his way in."

The decision was inevitable, the execution was hard. The band was lined up to appear at the second Mont De Marsan punk festival near Bordeaux in France, there was a recording session booked immediately afterwards, and Henry had been excited by the prospects. Stewart and Sting decided to bring Andy in, but to keep Henry until after the recording.

Andy wasn't exactly overjoyed, but he'd committed himself and couldn't back out. He made his irritation clear though. "Andy came in and said maybe three words to Henry during the entire time they were in the group together. He just vibed Henry right out," says Stewart.

The four-piece Police played their first gig at the Camden Music Machine in London at the end of July – "disastrous" according to Stewart – and their last a few days later at Mont de Marsan. As anticipated, Henry and Andy did not hit it off. "Andy was the ultimate guitar player. 'Do this! You can't? Oh ... '," says Henry. "I felt like the young fox being made to listen to the old wolf.

"At Mont de Marsan we had a stupid argument about an amplifier. Because he was the best guitar player he had to have the best amp ... it may sound bitter, but it's not. I went and got one, a Hiwatt, and went back to tell Andy he should hurry because there weren't many left. But he carried on practising his chords and finally all he could find was a small combo. To a man of his experience it should make no difference, but he came back and started to moan. Stewart says 'Andy's mad, why don't you give him the Hiwatt!'. So I did.

"Then when the Maniacs were on stage they blew an amp and dug out a really good Marshall to replace it. I asked if I could borrow that and when Andy saw it he went mad again. I looked at him, ten years older than me and telling me how to behave in life! I was really pissed off with that gig. I didn't see them afterwards. I went off with my girlfriend."

53

If Mont de Marsan was fraught, the recording session afterwards was even worse. They'd arranged to be produced by John Cale, the Welshman who'd founded the Velvet Underground with Lou Reed. Miles Copeland had brought him to the UK to work on Squeeze's debut album, but he was the wrong choice for the Police. "It was terrible," says Andy. "Punk was heavy in the air at that time and he was totally carried away with it. He couldn't take us on our own for what we were. He just wanted us to be an imitation punk band."

It may be a psychological blockage, but Andy can't remember Henry playing in the studio. Stewart can and has a very different view: "Cale knew during the sessions that we were going to fire Henry and he flipped. He said 'Whaaat? This new guitarist you've got is a load of crap!'. This was because Andy and Cale had immediately started arguing whereas Henry regarded him as a hero so they got along great."

"Cale didn't give a shit," says Henry. "He read the paper while we were playing. They all wanted to kill John Cale. They were sane and he was insane! Really though, he was just trying to bring up the adrenalin. At the end of the session I left with Sting. He was very depressed. He'd had a row with Cale over the vocals on 'Visions In The Night' although I thought he'd sung it really well after that. But you know how Sting is: he couldn't stand to be directed by somebody like John Cale. Anyway that was it for me.

"When I got home I talked to Stewart on the phone and he said it was all over. I went back to Corsica and had the most deserved holiday of my life. I'd done all I wanted in those months in London. I knew I would come back and be a musician."

Returning to London after two months Henry went straight into the guitarist's spot with the Electric Chairs who were better known then than the Police. Later he re-emerged with Nick Kent's Subterraneans and then with his own Flying Padovanis who released their first single in the spring of 1981.

Miles was still devoting precious little of his 20-hour-a-day work schedule to the Police. When he looked up from the affairs of Faulty to notice Andy's arrival in the band he was even less interested. "Miles took one look at Andy and said 'The guy's got short hair and bell bottoms'," Stewart recalls. "He'd had his hair cut, but he still hadn't bought a new pair of jeans."

Andy sensed the disapproval: "I heard that Miles didn't want me in the band and that immediately made me not want to have anything to do with him. I thought that Stewart was being over-influenced by his elder brother."

But Andy was a great help to Stewart: "Suddenly I was able to discuss things with somebody who knew what was going on. Before that I'd been the only one to say when to show up and which gigs we were going to play. Now there was Andy saying 'Wait a minute, what's this?'

"The other thing that happened was that Sting's ears pricked up. He started trying some of his Last Exit songs on Andy while we were rehearsing. He'd do it in a fit of daydreaming, sort of 'Remember music?'. This was while Andy was learning the set. One of the first things he said to me — maybe I imagined it but I seem to remember it — was 'I already know the set. E, A and D isn't it? Right'.

"Sting and I were quite indolent in our way. Sometimes we would say 'Oh fuck it, it'll be all right on the night' and Andy would say 'No, we must rehearse again tomorrow'. Andy's always the one to say 'Let's make that an hour earlier'. Even though you always land up waiting for him!"

The new trio made its debut at Birmingham's Rebecca Club on August 18. Andy says: "The first few times we played in public and pulled it off convinced me that it was there. But we were going round these punk places trying to maintain some identity and integrity. I felt pretty uncomfortable about that. Well, it was ridiculous for me wasn't it? It's one thing to identify with the spirit and the energy; it's another to pretend that you really are a punk. No way!"

However, suspicions of their punk pedigree had hardened and the trickle of bookings dried up. To British rock fans and promoters the Police were dead. Finally in mid-October 1977 they thought they'd fixed a series of European dates supporting Wayne County and the Electric Chairs again. They piled their guitars and one amp into Andy's Citroën Deux Chevaux and set off across the Channel to Rotterdam.

"When we got there we found there were no gigs at all," says Andy. "The promoter hadn't booked us. We met him and he had the Damned on tour so he said we could do some gigs with them. Then we drove down to Paris to link up with Wayne County after all. But that was a disaster. We went on at eight o'clock and the place was completely empty. Then my car broke down in the middle of Paris and we had to get it towed back to England. It was all a complete misery."

But not entirely fruitless. Sting took a stroll through the red-light district: "It was the first time I'd seen prostitution on the streets and those birds were actually beautiful. I had a tune going round in my head and I imagined being in love with one of those girls. I mean, they do have fellas. How would I feel?"

Roxanne
You don't have to put on the red light
Those days are over
You don't have to sell your body to the night
Roxanne

"It's a beautiful name and there's such a rich mythology behind it. Roxanne was Alexander the Great's wife and Cyrano De Bergerac's girlfriend. It has an emotive quality about it."

That was inspiration, but it wasn't money in the bank — yet. With the band at a low ebb Stewart acknowledges: "The women were supporting us. We didn't get a penny from anyone else." Frances was starting to get acting work to keep the Sting household solvent. One part in a television serial called *The Survivors* conveniently called for a mother and baby so Joseph found himself earning his crust as well. Kate Summers was working for an advertizing agency while Stewart's girlfriend Sonja was on a retainer from record producer Roy Thomas Baker although the planned album never materialized.

Meanwhile Stewart had sneaked into a sideline reviewing drumkits for *Sounds* magazine's technical pages. Indeed he managed to score his first Tama kit for free after a favorable review though in fairness, he has stuck with the brand ever since.

Sting was also moonlighting: "I paid the rent by doing modelling. I had an amazing career! The first job I ever went for I got. Pippa Markham sent me as a favor. It was a cinema ad for men's necklaces – gold chains with macho things hanging off them like signs of the Zodiac".

His career flourished with never a rejection: Brutus jeans, Triumph bras (he enjoyed that one: staring moodily at the camera while Triumph bra-clad models drifted around him). Later he auditioned for a Wrigleys' chewing gum commercial. They were looking for somebody punky and Sting is said to have convinced the director by leaping on a table and gobbing at him! When the agency told him they needed a group naturally he offered them the Police. Then they said: "There's just one thing, you have to be blond."

Sting already was, Stewart was actually red-headed at this point and game for anything, so Andy had to submit: "Hair is not really that big an issue I suppose. And in some ways it unified the group. Mind you, the first time I looked in the mirror I had this really brassy orange-yellow hair. I looked like some old whore! It took a bit of getting used to and of course the people I'd known before were all sniggering at me. It was pretty grim – no work, no money and bright blond hair."

Still, in October they were about to come into money, although not as the Police. When Andy joined the band he had one outstanding commitment: to record an album with Eberhard Schoener. He was able to rope Stewart in and at the end of their European 'tour' they went off to Munich leaving Sting to get the car towed back to England. When Andy and Stewart arrived they soon persuaded Eberhard to fly Sting out, and so the Police were assembled alongside an avant-garde orchestra.

They recorded with Eberhard for three weeks and then he asked them to come back the following year. The material was spread over two albums in Germany although for England it was condensed into one LP called 'Video Flashback', released in 1979, which took in some later pieces too.

Back in London at the beginning of November with substantial cheques in their pockets they decided that what the Police needed was a manager. "I decided I couldn't really handle the business side of it any more," says Stewart. "The accountant who'd been helping me with things like registering the name and getting a VAT number – we had that together although we weren't earning anything! – said to me one day 'I know this guy who's interested in managing you' and I said 'Someone who's interested in managing the Police? You're kidding'.

"He was a Persian called Alex Riahi. He said 'I'll give you £60 a week, I'll take care of promotion, I've got plenty of ideas'. He also had a rehearsal studio so we went there every day which was great, but there was no progress from him. No gigs, nothing.

"I'd say 'How about an agent? Are you getting anyone down to see us?'. He did actually get someone from the NEMS agency who sat there and said (*Stewart sniffs and adopts a Cockney accent*) 'Yeah, well, I can see the possibilities like but there's not many gigs arahnd at the moment. I'll tell you what, you need a record contract'. Which was exactly what we didn't want to hear. I know we've been praised as the band who wouldn't take a deal until it was the right one, but to be frank about it there weren't any wrong deals either.

"After about a month we decided that it wasn't happening so we loaded our equipment into the back of

Sting: "What we're trying to do as entertainers is maintain – or rather *achieve* – innocence. When I forget where I am, that's the best time. I feel very strongly that my work is to incite this quite conscious frenzy. It's very much my job out there to make people lose themselves. I like to appear on-stage as the victim of something, if you can understand that."

Andy's car and scarpered without saying a word."

At least they had rehearsed a new set for free. Spurred by the possibilities Andy had brought to the band Sting had been writing furiously: "There was constant pressure on from me. I was coming up with new songs all the time."

Ignoring their complete lack of gigs and placing their faith in 'Fall Out's' surprising success – sales had reached 10,000 – they decided to record an album and release it themselves on Illegal. "We figured that an LP would be better business than a single in terms of income per unit," says Stewart. "We worked out we'd need to sell 5,000 to cover our costs, which seemed a realistic target."

They needed money; more than they had. For the first time in the Police's life Stewart went to Miles and he agreed to lend them enough to pay the studio bills. Possibly against his better judgement, Miles was involved.

But first they broke for Christmas. Andy and Kate went to the States while Sting stayed at home and threw a huge New Year's party featuring Stewart's hi-fi and

Klark Kent caught in the act of destroying his short-lived popularity.

reggae collection; giving rise to the myth that this was the night Sting first heard reggae.

A few days later he went back to Newcastle for a Last Exit reunion at a jam-packed University Theatre. The differences which had led to the band's untidy breakdown almost a year earlier had been forgotten and they received a rapturous reception. It was Sting's first gig for over two months and he must have been wondering at the end what he had let himself in for.

But he didn't have time to brood on it. A week later the Police went down to Surrey Sound Studios to start work.

Surrey Sound, in Leatherhead, was the brainchild of Nigel Gray MD, a doctor who'd been unable to shake off rock 'n' roll and had finally submitted to his obsession instead of his profession. He and his brother had converted a small theater into a demo studio, picking up the expertize as they went along.

When the Police found the studio it had just been upgraded to 16-track and Nigel was eager to attract customers: "They liked the studio because it was big and very natural sounding. They came down and did a couple of tracks and were delighted. We were only about £10 an hour then. But if they'd thought it was cheap and crummy they'd have moved somewhere else."

Miles offered Nigel £2,000 on completion of recording or a percentage on sales of the album if he was prepared to wait. "But at that time we had everything on hire purchase," explains Nigel, "and we were broke. We just couldn't afford not to have the money. So I settled for the £2,000. The irony of it was that he didn't pay until much later and he didn't give me the percentage point either."

They started recording 'Outlandos D'Amour' in mid-January, 1978. Miles would occasionally drop by to check up on his investment: "The first time he came down they'd just done 'Be My Girl'," recalls Nigel. "He really laid into it. He called it hippy rubbish that Curved Air had done five years ago."

But his next visit was momentous. He met 'Roxanne'. Nigel explains: "We'd had trouble with that long pause between the verses. At first there were no vocals down so when they had to start each verse they weren't quite together. I would set the machine up to record, run through into the studio, stand on a cabinet and conduct them through to the end of each verse."

Miles's earlier crushing criticisms had put the band on the defensive. They thought the medium-paced tempo of 'Roxanne' would simply incur more of his wrath so they kept it back. However after they'd played the rest of the tapes Miles still looked distinctly unimpressed and, in desperation, they decided to give 'Roxanne' a whirl. Three minutes later Miles was converted. Fired with evangelical zeal he took a copy away, promising action.

Even the Faulty Products crew, to whom the Police were about as fashionable as joss-stick and kaftans, were bowled over. "That evening Miles came back from Surrey Sound with this demo tape and it was magic!" says Nick Jones. "We insisted that Miles give us a copy and we played it for two days continuously."

Next day Miles took the tape to A&M Records where he was something of a blue-eyed boy because Squeeze had just chalked up a couple of hits. He persuaded them to release 'Roxanne' as a single. When Miles relayed the news to the band they were elated. Suddenly somebody wanted to listen. The Police had to do an instant about-face from cursing Miles's indifference to applauding his vigor.

Sting says: "It was Miles masterminding our initial deal with the record company that gave us our freedom of movement. Once we got going we were unstoppable. We had 'Roxanne', which A&M thought was a left-field song which might happen. So Miles said 'You can have the single and we don't want any money in advance, we'll just have a better deal thank you'. That astonished them and they grabbed it because it meant no risk to them. The relationship with them grew from there. We started as equals so now we have an incredible deal with A&M — a great percentage. They owe *us* a fortune, exactly the opposite position to many groups who want success at any price so they sign away vast sums."

Miles's new-found enthusiasm for the Police soon had them playing live at last. They supported the American hippy band Spirit on three British dates in March which Miles had arranged. It was a strange combination, but the Police made the most of it. "We played really well and got the audience going," says Andy. "All the Spirit roadies were going up to Miles and saying how good we were. Miles hadn't actually committed himself to us with 'Roxanne' I don't think, but it came gradually. It was never 'I'm going to manage you!' or anything like that."

The identity of the Police was starting to take shape. They continued recording 'Outlandos' in two-day spurts throughout the first half of '78. A&M's acceptance of 'Roxanne' had given Sting a further impetus and soon afterwards he composed 'Can't Stand Losing You' which was a close rhythm relation. The label latched on to it, but showed their suspicion of what Nigel Gray candidly called his "amateur set-up" by trying to remix it themselves. However, they had to admit they couldn't improve on the original.

The Police shelved some of the earlier demos and used them on the B-sides of singles: 'Dead End Job', 'Landlord' and 'A Sermon' (an incomplete version of which turned up nearly three years later on the back of 'De Do Do Do De Da Da Da').

The white reggae element in their music — their 'regatta de blanc' — has been described as everything from a revolution to a rip-off. It was to cause a sensation and yet the band don't want to see it as a radical innovation. Sting insists: "Let's face it, the West Indian influence has always been there, particularly among jazz players. It wasn't invented by Bob Marley. You can go back to Millie (*'My Boy Lollipop', a British hit in 1964*), the Migil Five (*'Mockingbird Hill', again in 1964*) or even Cy Grant singing calypsos on TV. It's not as if we jumped on a bandwagon; we just adapted reggae for our own music.

"Think of those early songs I wrote with very obvious reggae parts in them. It was transparent what I'd done: written 16 bars of reggae and then 8 bars of standard rock 'n' roll, then back again, as simple as that. Join the two together and you've got 'Roxanne' and 'So Lonely'.

"That was what was in my mind, that you could set the two forms alongside each other and it would sound good, the pace would suddenly change. Then as we progressed the two styles merged. Now there's none of the stop-start thing, the songs have refined themselves into what's known as 'The Police Formula'."

Stewart had jammed around with reggae in Curved Air soundchecks with guitarist Mick Jacques: "I tried it in the early days of the Police too, but I didn't get any feedback and you can't play reggae with just drums. But I remember after Sting's New Year's Eve party we played more reggae in rehearsals. Then we started thinking of applying some of those licks to songs. We didn't just want to play reggae though. The Clash had already done that. So when we did 'Roxanne' I can remember trying to work out a different sound."

Stewart: "I know I'm red hot and all that but the Police would probably have been pretty successful with some drummer who could just hold the beat."

Andy sees reggae as no more than a departure point: "For us it was the blending of rock and reggae and punk, and using the spaces that reggae provides to find a fresh approach to playing as a three-piece, rather than just banging out heavy power chords all night long — although we do a bit of that too!"

'Roxanne' was released on April 7 and received favorable reviews but little radio play, partly because programers were reluctant to use a love song to a prostitute. Gigs were still as scarce as ever, so the return visit to Eberhard Schoener, who had lined up a concert season in a circus tent including a laser show, was financially welcome. "The whole concept was Eberhard's," says Stewart. "There was this girl singer doing kind of operatic jazz. When we were jamming around she'd say 'No, I'm only into jazz'. This got Sting going. He started singing too and within a few bars the whole show was revolving around him!"

In interviews a year or so later Eberhard tried to take the credit for 'teaching Sting to sing', but it's a claim that the band all hotly deny and with reason. Sting may learn, but he's never taught.

They came back to England early in June and paid off a few more bills, although they found that 'Roxanne' had got as far as the fringes of the Top Forty without quite making the breakthrough. The group were set for a lean and frustrating time. But Stewart's attentions were temporarily diverted from the Police when a character called Klark Kent emerged via Faulty Products with a single called 'Don't Care' on the previously unheard-of Kryptone label.

Stewart claimed to be a 'close personal friend' of the reticent and mysterious Mr Kent and took it upon himself to champion his cause. According to a Press release that accompanied the single, Kent first materialized in Llandyckkk, a Welsh fishing village where, despite only speaking a New Orleans patois, he became the church organist. It was the first in an increasingly bizarre sequence of events which was to culminate in New York at the height of his fame.

Stewart's handout averred that: 'His personal manners began to excite adverse attention following the unfortunate 'Lasagna Affair' when the beautiful eponymous triplets, stricken into sadness after he had rejected their sexual advances, threw themselves holding hands from the top floor of the Mobil Oil Building singing 'Ave Maria' before splashing themselves on to 42nd Street below. Kent, claiming he was the author of this traditional song, sued the grieving parents of the dead girls on the grounds that they had 'gained unwanted notoriety' for a song which he had written in some previous life and which, as he put it, "belongs to posterity and not to me". Some weeks later the *Daily News* ran a front page picture of Klark Kent urinating on the graves of the sisters, thus signaling an abrupt end to his short-lived popularity.'

Mr Kent's deranged character attracted the perverse attention of the music Press and the record began selling. Before long A&M took over distribution and pressed it in green vinyl. It reached the lower regions of the Top Forty at which point the BBC TV chart show *Top Of The Pops* asked Klark Kent to perform.

On the day of recording, a strange assortment of masked musicians arrived at the studio and created considerable confusion. Kent's manager, one Melvyn Milquetoast, was heard adopting the vocal mannerisms of Miles Copeland and the bass player spoke in husky Geordie tones. However Kent remained an enigma despite probing reporters spotting the fact that the single was recorded at Surrey Sound Studios and making logical deductions. The story went cold when the single failed to progress further. Years later *The Sun* newspaper claimed Kent was none other than Stewart Copeland, but who believes *The Sun*?

Sting was also about to flirt with another identity. He auditioned for his first film role, and, true to form, landed the part. It was in *Quadrophenia*, a version of the Who's concept album set in the heyday of the mods. Sting was to play the Ace Face, a mod gang leader. Filming was set for September.

Meanwhile A&M had by no means given up on the Police. They were convinced that 'Roxanne' had deserved a better fate so they decided to release 'Can't Stand Losing You' which came out on August 14. Again there were good reviews and no airplay. This time it was the suicide angle implied by the lyrics that caused program controllers to quake. The picture on the sleeve, showing Sting dangling from a noose, his feet scarcely touching a block of ice which was being melted by an electric fire, probably didn't help either.

Nevertheless A&M took up an option to release 'Outlandos'. The group delivered the tapes and that was the day they became 'rich'. At least that's how Stewart felt: "They gave us a cheque for £10,000. We split it up on the spot and that afternoon I went into Faulty with a new pair of jeans and some albums under my arm. That lump of money sitting in my bank account! I felt in a different world." Not that it would look like much of a fortune when they'd paid their debts.

But at last some more gigs came their way, supporting another of Miles's punk protégés Chelsea on tour, and they recorded a session for Radio One's influential *John Peel Show*.

Through all these fits and starts the group kept their music moving. One important factor was Kim Turner who had arrived as the group's road manager and soundman. He had turned 'business-minded' since Cat Iron days and for a while he'd co-managed the Cortinas with Miles who then offered him 25 per cent of the Police's management.

"I didn't do the sound at the start," says Kim. "I used various PA companies. I'd be sitting there thinking 'The sound on the guitar is crap, and I can't hear Sting's voice'. I didn't know anything about mixing, but I'd go up and say 'It's not sounding right' and if the guy still messed it up I'd start fiddling with the knobs until I got what I wanted. I just learnt by doing it. Then when Andy bought an echo unit for his guitar I really got interested and started to use one on Sting's voice, then Stewart's drums too. It was a whole new texture."

As their musical character grew, recognition came. They had fans! Stewart noticed it for the first time at the Marquee Club in August. But their followers had little opportunity to follow. A band with two failed singles hardly inspired confidence among agents and promoters. Dead end job...

Then Miles came back from America with a proposition.

6
BLOOD AND GUTS AND GROTTY MOTELS

Miles Axe Copeland 3's plan was that the Police should go over to America and play a series of club dates around the East Coast. It was against all the 'rules' of promoting British bands in the States but Miles had been preparing the ground with brother Ian, who had moved to America early in 1978, having gone as far as he could in the British agency scene. He'd joined the Paragon agency in Macon, Georgia, and organized tours for Southern rock bands like Charlie Daniels and Marshall Tucker. But he wanted to develop punk.

"The new wave was anti-establishment and the American bigwigs didn't want to know because it threatened their existence," explains Ian. "And the resistance got more entrenched because every time they'd hear a new British band they realized that they were that much more obsolete. Either the record company decided you were going to be a hit and ploughed a lot of money in for you to come over and promote the record, or they didn't and you stayed home."

To break this rock 'n' roll version of Catch 22, Ian put together a circuit of clubs on the East Coast between Washington DC and Toronto, each within driving distance of the next. "We were looking for a break-even figure of 200 dollars a night. That was easy to get out of a club because it was what they paid their local bands. I'd call up and they'd say 'We can't afford your touring bands'. So I'd say 'How much do you pay your local bands?'. 'A coupla hundred bucks'. 'Fine, I'll take it'.

"They couldn't work out how I could do it but it was possible if everyone traveled in the van with the equipment and you stayed in double rooms at Travel Lodges for 20 dollars a night. Every now and again there would be a 500-dollar gig in New York or Boston and that would pay for a day off along the way."

Miles and Ian tried out the circuit in the summer of 1978 with Squeeze who'd just had an English hit, 'Take Me I'm Yours'. They represented the 'acceptable face' of the British new wave – they looked presentable and they could play well – so A&M were induced to provide $8,000 worth of support. Miles remembers: "When I brought Squeeze over the initial reaction was 'Oh God, a punk band!' but when they met them it was 'Hey, they're really nice guys', and they got to play at the A&M convention. So we dispeled the notion that new wave bands couldn't play and that they were all offensive.

"The tour still lost money but the promoters at the clubs were asking us for more bands like that. The Police tour was the first one we did completely on our own, although we talked Paragon into helping. They lent me some money to buy a van, which we paid back over a period of time. Ian drove it up from Macon to New York with the amplifiers."

The Police flew over on October 20, 1978, on Freddie Laker's Skytrain carrying their instruments as hand luggage. "We arrived in New York at eleven o'clock at night and we were supposed to be onstage at CBGB's by midnight," says Andy. "We rushed there from the airport and found these terrible amplifiers on stage but we just plugged in and got on with the set. It was fantastic."

The tour consisted of 23 gigs in 27 days and took in such exotic locations as Poughkeepsie, Willimantic, Swissvale and Centerville as well as New York, Philadelphia, Boston, Detroit, Cleveland, Toronto, Buffalo and Washington. It grossed a total of 7,142 dollars.

"We really felt as if we were pioneering: it was us against the system," Andy says. "But we attracted a fair amount of attention because we had a novelty value. The radio stations heaved a sigh of relief because they could actually play 'Roxanne' and feel up-to-date. The audiences took us more seriously than people in England because they weren't so prejudiced and would accept us if we had the right record. But we did feel very different; the support was always some band with platform heels and long hair playing heavy metal.

"But the most important thing was that we played continuously for nearly four weeks. We'd never done that before. It pulled us together. And there was a reaction too. That's what you need – unless you get a response, what's the point?"

But Sting, in America for the first time, reckons it was harder going than that: "Miles and Ian had made the plan of campaign but we were the troops who went out there and gave our blood and guts, staying in grotty motels and driving round in the wagon. We'd travel 400 miles to Poughkeepsie and find that literally three people were there. Getting it up for three people was quite an experience. We did it though, we were very good for three people. But we all knew the potential. That's what kept us going. Touring America was on the way up. We had reached the nadir well before that – six months of not working at all."

Kim Turner, who was the entire road crew for the tour, was well aware of the opposition the band faced from the record company: "A&M called up Ian and said 'What the hell are you doing bringing this group into the country? We're not giving you any tour support, you guys are crazy'. But Ian said 'We don't want your money. We want you to release 'Roxanne' and be nice enough to get a few promotion men to come and see the band'.

"At that time the motto was 'If you want a job done, do it yourself'. There was none of this 'I'm a musician, I'm not a roadie' sort of thing. We would go around putting up posters ourselves. I'd get into a town and call the radio stations and hassle the guys to come down to the gig."

Apart from the Poughkeepsie fiasco where, as Ian says, "instead of introducing themselves, the band introduced the audience to each other", there were no serious mishaps on the tour. "If they'd been of a mind to I'm sure they could have made every one a disaster," he adds. "They could have looked at any lousy dressing-room and said 'I ain't playing this place'. But instead it would be 'Well, maybe if we move this old piano off stage we'll be able to get the drumkit on' or whatever. They had as much determination to make something out of nothing as I did."

The reward came quickly. 'Roxanne' was played a lot on the radio on the East Coast. By the time they came back to New York in the middle of November the single was rising up the charts. In high spirits the Police returned

Sting in *Radio On*.

to Britain where A&M had released 'Outlandos D'Amour'. The reviews were moderate, sales were steady, but their low-budget approach meant that they recouped their costs quite soon.

Andy got back just in time to become a father: "Kate was seven and a half months pregnant when I left for that tour and all the time I was sweating. There she was on her own with that huge belly. I think she breathed a sigh of relief when I came back and she delivered a girl, Layla.

"It was a real emotional tightrope trying to look after Kate, Layla and the Police. But Kate and I felt that we wanted a baby and this was the time that we should have it, regardless of anything else that was going on, so we got on with it. I liked the getting on with it bit!"

But it was time to get on with something else. The band had the support slot on a tour with Alberto Y Lost Trios Paranoias, a satirical British band. "In England we hadn't really played outside London and we were a bit unsure of ourselves," says Andy. "We played the first night at Bath University and about 1,000 kids turned up. We went on first and the audience sounded as if they'd all come to see us. We were just completely blown away. All these kids were there because of 'Roxanne' and 'Can't Stand Losing You'. The records had obviously made a great impact even if they hadn't hit the charts. We did a dozen or so dates around England and the reaction was the same everywhere; it was just so emphatic. It was embarrassing in a way because the Albertos had to play second fiddle to us even though they were headlining."

Not that there was any money coming in. Kim Turner was required to use all his 'diplomacy' as tour manager to keep the band solvent: "We were on £50 a night. At every gig the sound man hassled me for £10 towards the use of the PA and I told him the Albertos manager had said it was for free, so I never gave him a penny. We traveled in a Transit van and I got a mate of mine to help out with the equipment. We stayed in the most ridiculous hotels. I'd got a list of guest houses for £2 a night which were down the road from the Holiday Inns where the Albertos were staying. So it was £10 a night for rooms, £10 a day for petrol and £10 for the roadie. Which left the four of us with enough to buy our food and splash out on the occasional set of strings and drumsticks."

Immediately after Christmas, Stewart's hunger for playing led him into the studio with Brian James, a guitarist who'd quit the Damned shortly before. Kim Turner played bass and the single, 'Ain't That A Shame', came out on Illegal Records. Early in January, James had a gig at the Electric Ballroom in London and Stewart and Kim played with him. Then, as Andy and Sting had turned up as well, the punters got an unannounced Police set to boot.

The band had agreed to play more concerts with Eberhard Schoener and spent most of January in Germany although by then it was starting to seem like an interruption to the Police's progress.

Within a couple of weeks of their return they were back at Surrey Sound working on their second album. "We were really hot from playing on the road and I think the recording reflected that," says Andy. The studio had just gone 24-track but Nigel believes the band's choice wasn't approved of by A&M. "They felt we weren't

Sting, the Ace Face in *Quadrophenia*.

professional enough at the studio and shouldn't be trusted with the company's 'big hope'. They thought we'd just been lucky first time. But the Police were adamant that they should come here and that just the four of us should do it."

They recorded 'Regatta De Blanc' in a total of four weeks running through to the summer. It cost between £6,000 and £9,000 (depending on who you talk to) which was easily covered by the profits from 'Outlandos'. It meant they could maintain their independence from A&M who would doubtless have preferred to foot the bills and exert a measure of control.

"We wanted to do it fast and cheap and still try and achieve superior results," Andy says. "We were trying to embody a lot of the new wave beliefs while a lot of the so-called punk groups weren't doing that at all. I mean, the Clash have spent much more money on making albums than we ever have."

The raw material for 'Regatta' was in a different form from 'Outlandos' according to Nigel: "They'd only played one or two of the songs live before and all the rest were demos. So they'd record their first impressions and then we'd discuss how to treat it." They weren't in a position to discard many songs either. They had to work at what they had. Andy remembers that they even considered re-recording 'Fall Out' at one point.

But if quantity was lacking, quality certainly wasn't. One of the first songs proffered by Sting was 'Message In A Bottle', another milestone for the band. Andy traces its evolution: "Sting had that riff for a while, but there was another tune with it originally. He'd been fiddling about with it during our first American tour. Finally he rearranged the riff slightly and came up with the song."

It fired Stewart to produce what each of the band regards as the finest piece of drumming he's recorded. "'Message In A Bottle' was a dead cert hit from the first attempt at a backing track," he says.

Nigel Gray had become adept at spotting the sound the Police were looking for: "'Walking On the Moon' has two guitar parts, but there are long gaps in it where you'd expect an extra guitar to fill in – and there's nothing, just the groove. They get the backing track, add the vocals and one or two overdubs, then have the faith to leave it. If anyone else had recorded 'Walking On The Moon' it wouldn't have been a hit – it's what the Police do to it that makes it special."

Stewart confirms: "'Walking On The Moon' took us a lot of work. It started out as a rocker but we finally changed it right around." The band were becoming increasingly aware of what Nigel calls their "characteristic trademarks". Stewart cites the title track of the album as an example: " 'Regatta De Blanc' came about when we started jamming with 'Roxanne' on stage. Then it solidified and became a little number in its own right, like a catchphrase almost. So we recorded it that way."

Andy was most aware of these trademarks and set about stamping a few more on the group's musical personality through his new custom-built pedal board which opened up a whole range of sounds on his guitar. "Gradually the sound started to become part of the content instead of just being an embellishment," he says. "Songs like 'Walking On The Moon' or 'Deathwish' wouldn't be the same without the guitar effects. To me that's perfectly valid. The technology is available and I enjoy using it. I was getting all these silvery sounds and when we started combining that with the reggae rhythms, the musical spaces, Sting's voice and more sophisticated chords it sounded more like the 1980s, not 1965. It took a while to find all these things. We'd pick them up by instinct and feeling and then realize what we were doing and start developing it more consciously."

'Regatta' wasn't to be released until the autumn. But in February 1979 the Police were about to erupt. As Miles Copeland likes to put it: "The nucleus was developed to a point where it would reach critical mass and explode." They hit the road and stayed on it for the next 16 months.

A concert at Hatfield was filmed for BBC's *Rock Goes To College* series which sustained their British presence while they went back to America where 'Roxanne' and 'Outlandos' had sprung into the charts. This had transformed the Police from no-hopers to contenders within two months and they played over 30 dates across the States.

Sensing that British interest in the band was picking up, A&M tried again with 'Roxanne'. They re-released it on April 12 and by the time the Police came back for a short break from America it was already in the Top Thirty and they appeared on *Top Of The Pops* which helped it on its way to Number Twelve. In the wake of 'Roxanne', 'Outlandos' was towed into the LP charts six months after its release.

They didn't tour Britain again until June and by then demand for tickets was such that many of the dates were switched from clubs to larger halls. The ghoulish support act the Cramps from California were the first of several US new wave bands to be spotted by the Police on their travels and taken up by Miles and Ian.

The Police set was still based around 'Outlandos' and only 'Message In A Bottle' was getting a preview. When A&M put out 'Can't Stand Losing You' again to exploit the tour the band was even heard grumbling because it looked as though their recording career was becoming a bizarre re-run of '78. But the discontent was cut short when the single reached Number Two early in August, thwarted only by the Boomtown Rats' 'I Don't Like Mondays'. "We had to put that right next time," says Stewart competitively.

Sting didn't mind repeating a year: "It was no skin off our nose. We were playing the same set but the venues

---

Miles Copeland: "You need money to be idealistic."

were better. And we would have been playing our singles anyway. 'Roxanne' was going down great every night. The first time it came out in England it only sold 10,000 copies, the same as 'Fall Out'. When it was a hit the public didn't have a clue that it was a re-release. We got back from America thinking they'd forgotten us and we were heroes. It was lovely."

And so was Sting. The image of him on *Top Of The Pops* mock-miming while he swung his mike-stand around two feet from his right ear was a blatantly honest send-up of the program's commercial rigmarole. Seduction by charm.

As 'Outlandos' went 'gold' in the UK for sales over 100,000 copies the band went to Europe for a series of headlining concerts and then returned to England late in August to top the bill at the annual three-day Reading Festival in front of 20,000 people. A year earlier they'd have been happy to have a hundredth of that audience. To be life-size in that vast setting you have to be larger than life and Sting was magnificently intimate.

"We'd really started to pick up speed then," recalls Andy. "We could all feel it. There was something new happening every day and we'd have to work on it together. There was this tremendous thrust."

It was irresistible. In September, 'Message In A Bottle' came out, their first 'new single' for over a year, and two weeks later they had the Number One they'd been craving. The week after, 'Regatta De Blanc' was released they found themselves simultaneously top of the album and single charts. The date was October 9.

A British tour on the heels of their Reading Festival triumph showed that Sting could handle opposition as well as adulation: "Fifty skinheads broke into the theater at Oxford. They knocked over an old lady and a doorman and ploughed their way through the audience going 'Sieg heil, sieg heil' to the front of the stage. The bouncers melted away and they got on stage. The problem was that I had to make fools of them and at the same time make it appear that I was one of them. It was like dancing with bears but I used them – 'Come on, you're on stage, let's see you work' – and I made them dance. It was a victory. No one got hurt. That was largely a result of my teaching experience: divide and conquer. There were fifty skinheads on stage who'd been intent on destroying the gig actually contributing to it."

Mod was the fashion Sting was associated with however. *Quadrophenia* had just opened and the publicity surrounding Sting as the Ace Face was out of all proportion to his part. It was, as he admits, the perfect role: "Long enough to make an impact but not long enough to blow it.

"The film came out just as we had our first Number One. The whole thing seemed to be orchestrated but really it just fell together. Serendipity! I've no respect for the mod movement whatsoever, even when it was contemporary in the 60s, much less the half-hearted attempt at reviving it. I just played a part in a film." And wore a parka on stage at Reading!

He was the Ace Face on celluloid. He was The Face on the posters, the TV, the front page. You couldn't walk past a news stand without being stared at by him. He had developed an almost magical ability to be photogenic: "It started when I was about 25 I think. I decided that I could impose beauty on myself. As a result of a feeling . . . that it should be. It's a strange thing to talk about. But there is an expression I have. Seductive, serious." A camera swings his way and he flicks his fingers through his hair to check its informal tousle, sucks in his cheeks lightly, makes the smallest kink of a frown. The Sting look.

The mass media had recognized it. They used it. He used them. The Police were raised from rock stars to superstars.

But not yet in America. Oddly, the country where the Police had made their first impression had gone cool on them. During their two-month autumn tour there, the biggest they'd yet attempted, 'Regatta De Blanc' and 'Message In A Bottle' evoked no more than mild interest. There was no sign of escalation on the British scale.

But at least they had one captive audience. While in California they fitted in a concert at the Terminal Island Prison and raised 4,000 dollars to buy musical instruments for the inmates – a charitable idea they were to extend later.

The US tour went far beyond the club circuit Ian Copeland had originally devised, although that network was still being used for other new English bands like Ultravox and 999 to play the States and make money. Ian had extended it so that a group could gig its way from one side of the country to the other in a van with the venues spaced at 200 to 300-mile intervals, apart from one sizeable hop across the Rockies.

Miles and Ian had proved with the Police that it was possible to break unknown British bands in America without putting themselves in debt to record companies and were determined to capitalize on it. It was all part of the crusading, frontiersman spirit that was an indomitable part of the Copeland make-up.

Ian was still working for the Paragon agency but that autumn, out of the blue, its parent company Capricorn Records went bust, dragging the successful agency down with it. Ian found himself without an office, three bands on the road and a pregnant wife, Connie. It called for some fast maneuvering but Ian and Miles did it, setting up their own agency in New York. They christened it FBI – Frontier Booking International, what else?

If the band were getting a little despondent as they trekked round the States, the news from the UK was ecstatic. 'Walking On The Moon' was released as a single in November and shot to Number One. And even 'Fall Out', re-released by Faulty, sold enough to sneak a chart placing. While the Faulty staff had no direct connection with the Police they found themselves increasingly sucked in as Miles's preoccupation grew.

Sting had another cameo role in the movies too. This time it was a three minute spot as a garage attendant in *Radio On*, most of which he spent sitting in a caravan doorway strumming an acoustic guitar and singing Eddie Cochran's 'Three Steps To Heaven'. He'd also played a part in the Sex Pistols film *The Great Rock 'N' Roll Swindle* but mercifully his bit was edited out before that cinematic débâcle reached the screens.

The day after the Police's American tour, at the beginning of December, the band flew straight to Paris to begin a series of European dates and crammed in another dozen British shows before Christmas. It was then that they suddenly realized they'd stumbled on another market they'd hardly considered: the 'teenybopper' age-group between 11 and 15. The Police were

Sting: "We're all close. We fight each other and we fight for each other."

the unlikely successors to the Bay City Rollers and David Cassidy, the difference being that it had happened by accident rather than by slick, cynical manipulation.

The first date at Leeds Queens Hall produced scenes of mass hysteria. Security men hauled over 80 'unconscious' girls from the teeming, screaming throng. Many of them miraculously recovered to open their eyes for a prime view of Sting as they were carried past the stage on their way to the first aid center.

The band were astonished. Andy says: "We never thought we'd get that kind of teenage audience. I never felt that we compromised at all. Some of our music is definitely not teenage oriented. But I don't mind. You get a tremendous amount of enthusiasm with kids of that age; it's not all serious nodding of the head."

Sting, who was the subject of most of this pubescent adulation, reacted instantly: "We saw it just as it was about to happen. As it started to come over the hill I thought 'Yeah!' and went for it. When we were rehearsing for months on end without a gig we never thought about it. We just wanted to be a group making Top Ten records. To a lot of people teenyboppers are a sub-species not even to be entertained. I don't agree. If you can transcend the screaming you can take a generation with you into something else. It's a real challenge."

Propelled by the fever-pitch reaction at every concert, the group hauled themselves through their tenth tour of the year, the highlight of which came when they played two different venues in London on the same night – the seated Hammersmith Odeon and the standing-only Hammersmith Palais – travelling the quarter mile between the two in an armoured personnel carrier. And they still had enough energy to slot in a charity show at Lewisham at the end of the tour. The price of a ticket was a toy and the resulting pile was handed over to Dr Barnardo's orphanages.

By the end of the tour there were signs that the organization was starting to get a little stretched. The size of halls they were now filling meant that the entourage of band, tour manager and roadie was no longer sufficient. Sting was going to need protection from his fans as well.

There were a few compensations however. During 1979 the Police sold five million singles and two million albums. They'd taken over. A lot of people even thought the Police were the police: A&M Records received a letter from Eldon Griffiths, Member of Parliament and Parliamentary Consultant to the Police Federation, saying they had received hundreds of applications to join the Police Fan Club and asking if the group would be available to play the Federation's Annual Ball.

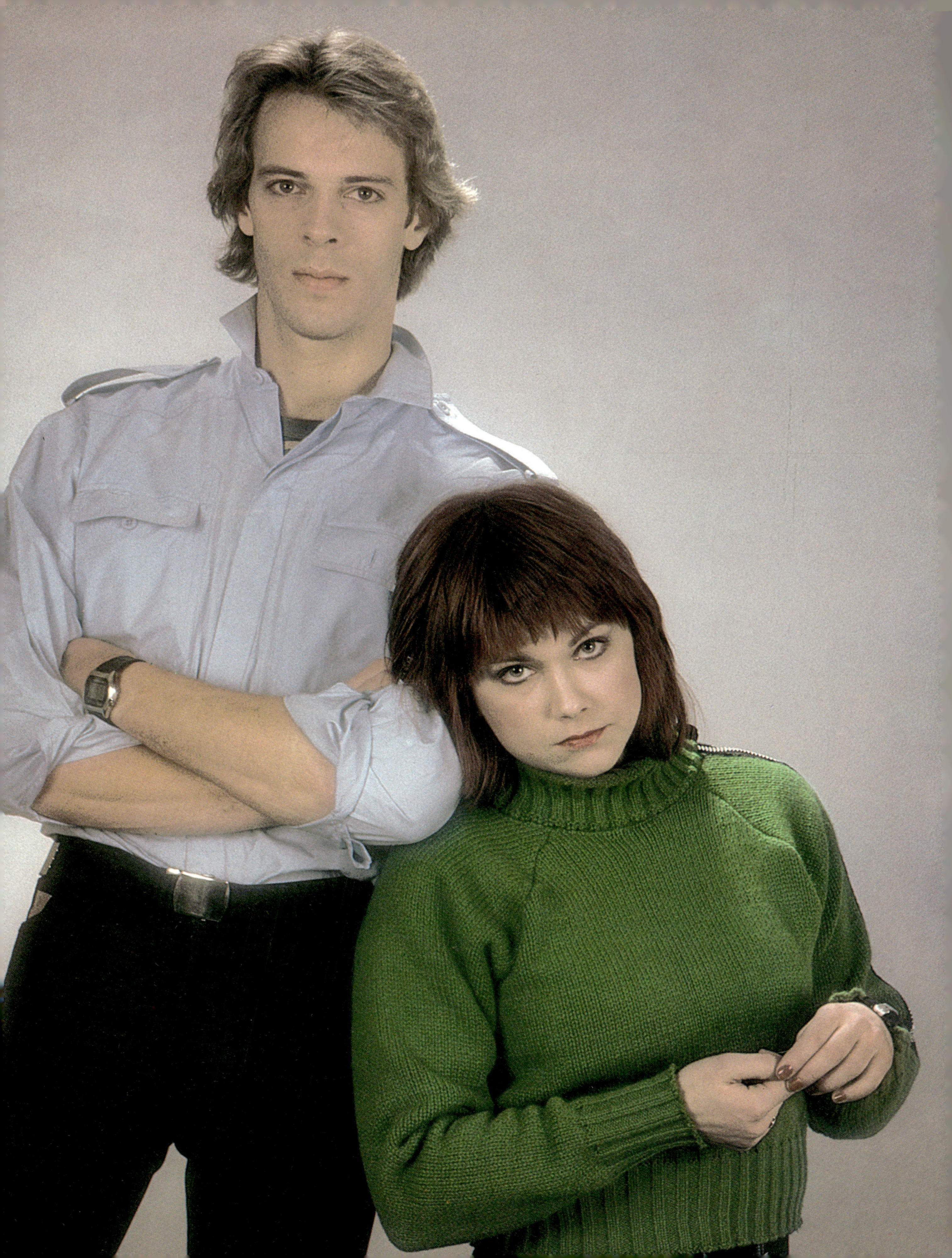

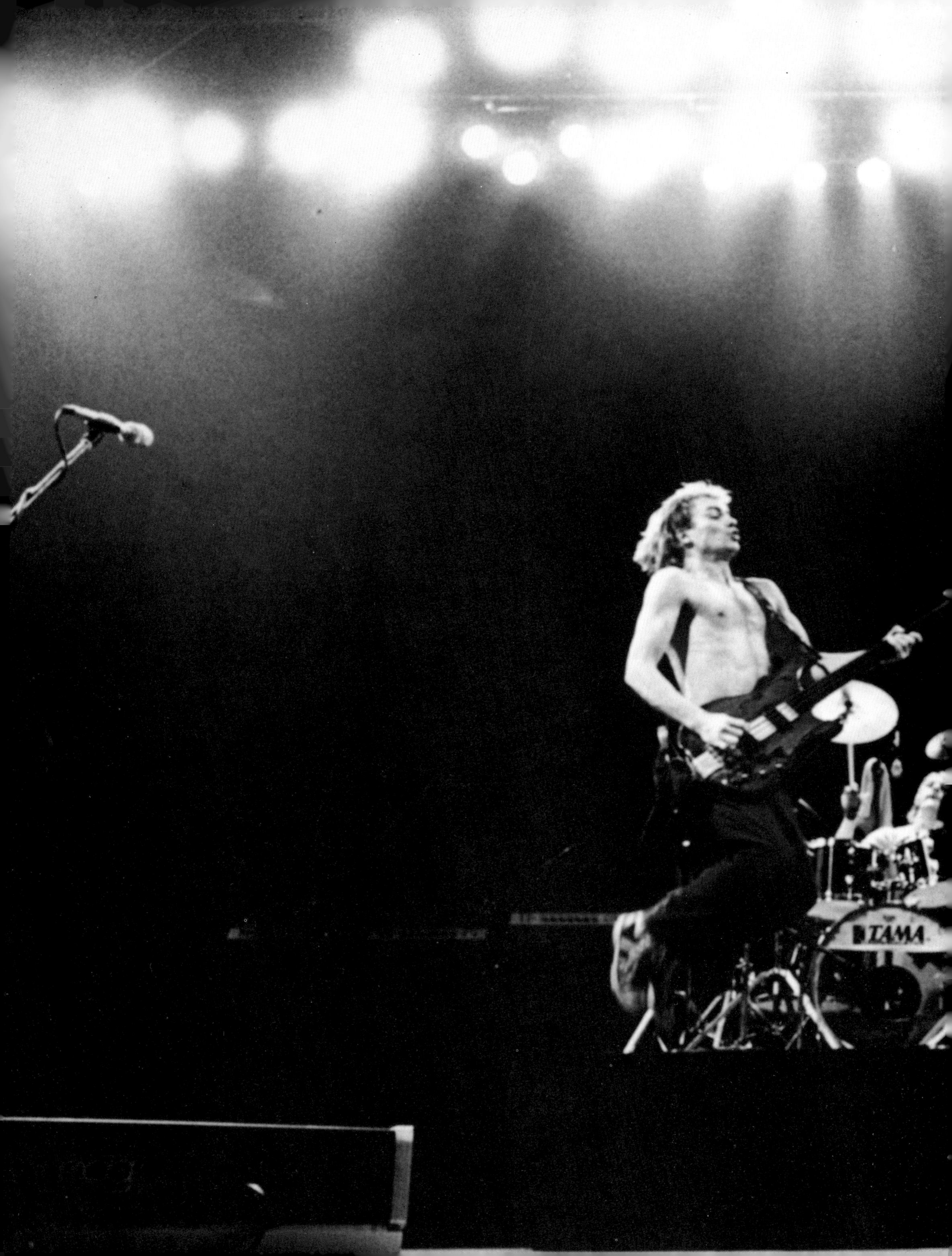
TAMA

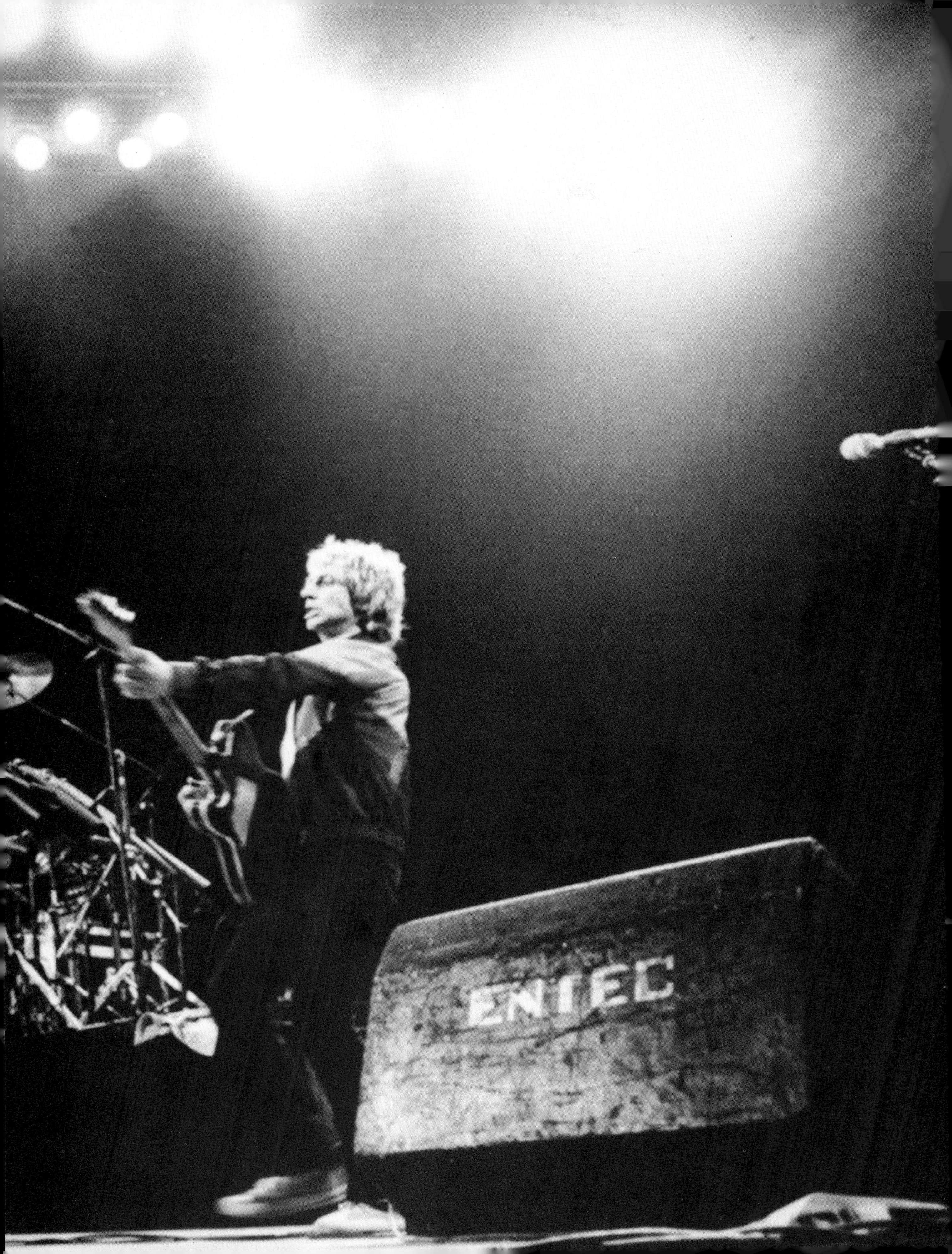
ENTEC

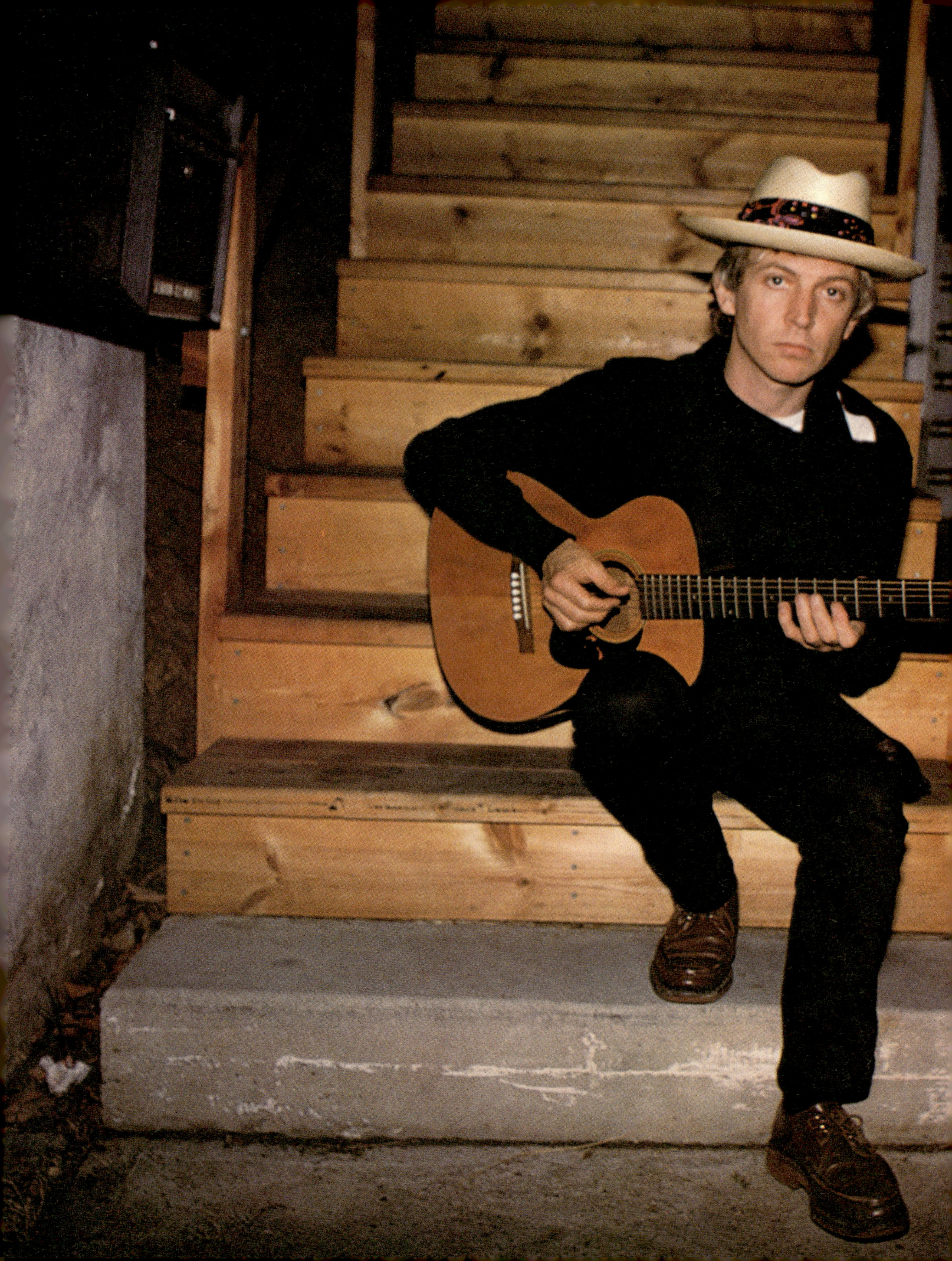

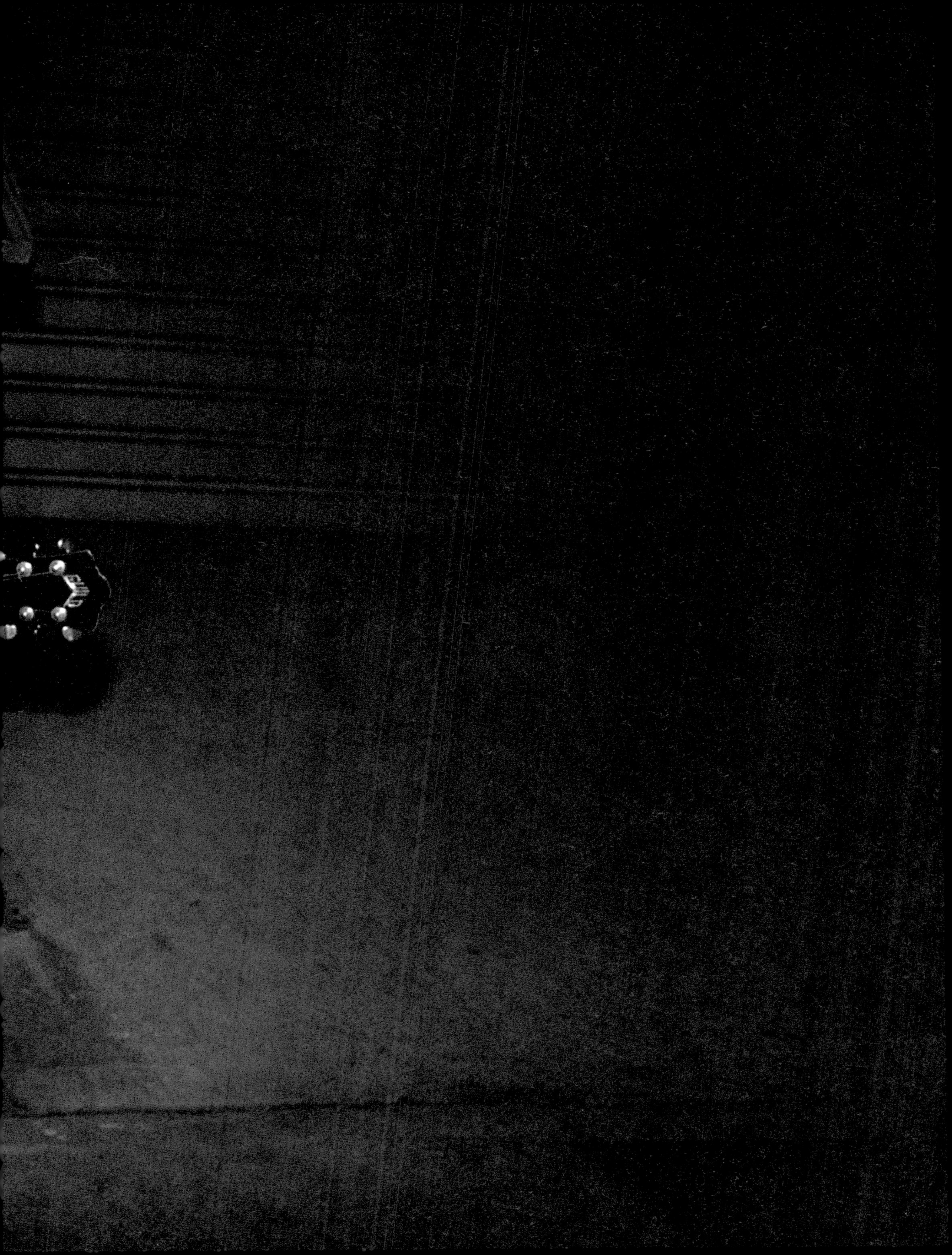

7

WORLD TOUR: EVEN THE SHEEP RIOTED

The UK was conquered. They had a bridgehead in America. But Miles Copeland had a global strategy. A real world tour on a scale that no one had attempted before.

"Most groups wait until their career is over before they go outside the States and Europe," Miles declares. "I say the energy of the Police is *now*. Let's take them to the rest of the world when they're at their most impressive. Let's have the whole world selling for us for the next ten years."

It could be his father talking when he reflects: "If all the Indians and all the Russians and all the Chinese get into Western music it means really that they get into Western culture which means that they become oriented towards the West as opposed to the East. But we're not doing it for any ulterior motive on my part. We're going to have fun!"

During the band's last American tour Miles had nipped off to a few exotic locations to test the possibilities. He had, after all, studied world development. Stewart shares the family view: "We Copelands know for a fact that there's a whole world out there, whereas other people may just have read about it. Until you actually go there it really doesn't exist.

"The other reality is that sooner or later the Third World is going to get its share. We in the West are such a minority with all our riches. However little you've got out of life here, compared with the vast majority of the earth's population you're stinking rich — fat, bloated and fed."

For Andy, going to countries that he'd never visited before was a challenge that would keep the band from getting jaded: "It worked on a number of levels. The traveling was invigorating and the fact that we could go and actually play gigs was a semi-historical feat.

"I didn't really take it all that seriously as a marketing enterprise. It cost us a lot of money to go to India and Egypt and we spent most of what we'd earned in America doing that. The main reward was the amount of publicity we got out of it which may have helped enlarge our myth. I was just proud of doing it."

Sting's oft-quoted remark that "We'll be able to find some interesting ethnic music to rip off" was meant as a humorous retort to journalists accusing the Police of being the latest bunch of Caucasians to plagiarize black music for commercial gain. But he did see the world tour as a chance to emulate the Beatles' world domination in the 60s.

They were scheduled to start in Japan in February 1980, but under the Copeland theory that you should never fly over a country if you can play in it, more American gigs were lined up along the way. Japan has an established rock scene and their first foray into the unknown came when they stopped off in Hong Kong and played in front of 500 people in a club en route for New Zealand and Australia, where Sting contracted laryngitis, forcing the band to postpone their concerts for a week.

India had the most profound effect on the band, particularly Sting: "I saw a lot of poverty and what *we* call degradation. I didn't see any despair. If you walked through Moss Side in Manchester you'd see more real despair.

"The greatest gig of my life was in Bombay. They'd never seen a rock concert so there was no element of ritual, no preconceptions. It was organized by the Time And Talents Club of Bombay which is a group of old ladies who put on charitable jumble sales. We did the concert in aid of sick children and raised about £5,000.

"We sold out a 5,000-seater open air arena in the middle of Bombay. It caused enormous media interest because we were a curiosity even though they'd never heard of 'the Police'. There were these huge crowds outside, many of whom were just curious to see what was going on. When we soundchecked they wanted in. They thought the concert had started. There was a mini-riot and the police went in with batons flying. Finally they let the ticket holders in, people like the Chief of Police — we always attract the Chief of Police! — the Lord Mayor, high-caste Hindus and sophisticated Bombayites.

"Then, to stop the trouble outside they opened the gates and in came Bombay. So we were faced with a cross-section of Indian society, beggars, everyone! People with tickets were saying 'Please sit down, I paid for this seat, why are you standing in front of me?'.

"When we came on I said politely 'Look, this is essentially dance music so please get up', and they did. They

Stewart: "The American Dream is how anybody with any kind of anything can actually make it from anywhere to anywhere. Social mobility is very easy; you can cross the structure and actually make it. In Britain it's very much more difficult. That's why it's called the American Dream and not the British Dream."

were very accommodating, even the old ladies in saris and umbrellas. But at the end of the gig we had another invasion by the 'lower elements of society' and there was another police charge with batons. This was just a week after they'd quelled a demonstration by blind people in the same brutal way, so I was making all kinds of pompous noises about 'give a man a baton and he's got to hit someone'. But it was an incredible gig. Emotional beyond belief."

For the Indian and Egyptian concerts the Police trimmed down their equipment to what Miles calls their 'combat rig' but the entourage was larger than usual because they were followed by at least one film crew throughout the world jaunt. *The Police In The East* TV documentary was being shot by Derek and Kate Burbidge who had made all the group's promotional videos.

The Burbidges and their crew encountered a few hazards along the way like getting trampled underfoot in Japan when the audience stormed the stage and having to cope with bolshy sheep in Australia. "The sheep rioted when Sting sang to them," says Kate. "They shat all over the studio and then jumped out of the pen. You'd be surprised how high a sheep can jump! But Stewart did better than we did. He kept up with it with his own movie camera."

India provided its own problems: "We arrived and were told there were very good lights. In fact there were four! The guy had said 'They're all different colors' but the 'colors' turned out to be crumpled tissue paper." But Kate's lasting memory is of the audience: "I remember all these dignitaries and old ladies sitting right at the front. I suggested they should move back because they would find it much too loud but they said it would be a disgrace for them to do that."

A more serious problem for the group came when they landed in Cairo. It was solved in classic Copeland style. Ian was there: "We arrived on Friday for a Saturday concert but we forgot that Friday is like Sunday in the West and everything was closed. The customs men locked the equipment away.

"Miles called our father in Washington and he told him the name of someone to get in touch with (*it was the former Nasser bodyguard who had been their next door neighbor in the 50s*). The next thing we knew, Mrs Sadat had personally authorized the customs to open up and the concert went ahead as planned."

Almost, except that Sting nearly landed up in jail. "During the gig there was this guy in plain clothes throwing people back into their seats," Sting remembers. "I yelled at him 'Fuck off! Who invited you?'. He still wouldn't go away and started threatening me so I said 'See him? Fill him in'' and all these kids piled into him. Well, he was the head of the Cairo police and I was in One Of My Moods.

"Afterwards Miles came back ashen-faced and said 'Ummm, he demands an apology'. I said 'Fuck off' and Miles said 'Sting, please, *please*'. Then this guy came into the room and stood there waiting, just looking at me. His

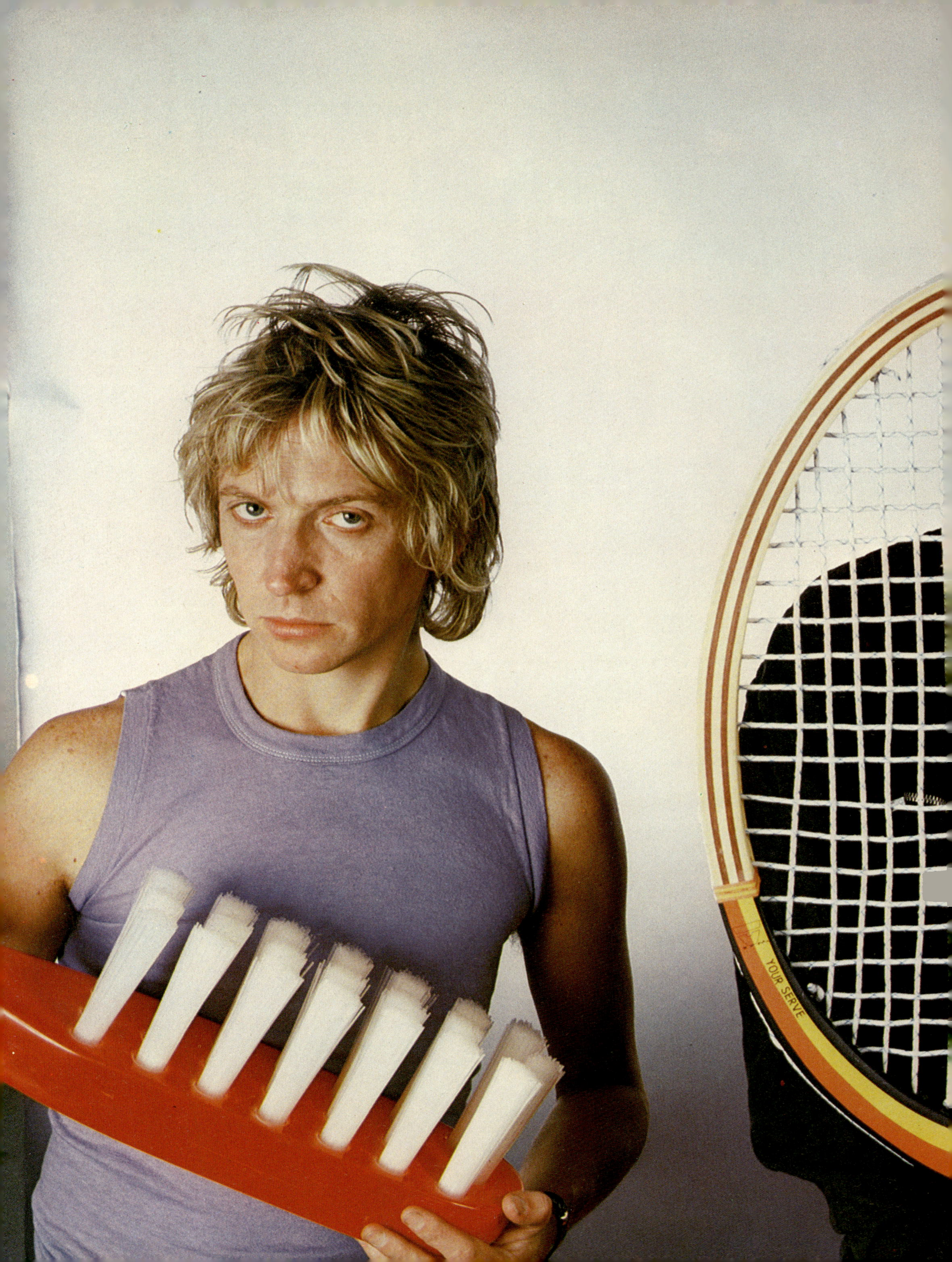
YOUR SERVE

WOOD
MADE BY THE WORLD'S LARGEST MANUFACTURER OF TENNIS RACKETS

Stewart: "The Police are exploiting the multiverse."

honor had been damaged. I couldn't do it so I got my bag and walked out. He followed me all the way to the car breathing down my neck so I realized I'd have to apologize otherwise I'd be in prison. I turned around and literally choked on the words. I could *not*. Then Miles jumped in and said 'What Sting means is that he's terribly terribly sorry'. The guy said 'You're a man of honor. I accept your apology' and walked away. That's the kind of person I am. I cannot accept somebody else's ascendency and power."

Fortunately, everybody kept their temperaments under control for the next part of the trip in Greece and Italy where rock concerts can be tempestuous affairs. Greece hadn't seen a British rock band since the Rolling Stones in 1967 and the police presence for the show in Athens was formidable, but the only trouble occurred outside the hall when fans with tickets were brusquely locked out. The same thing happened in Italy.

The final leg of the tour covered more familiar European countries, although they did take advantage of Spain's liberalization to play in Barcelona. They rounded off the trip at the beginning of May with a homecoming gig for Sting in Newcastle.

Maybe the accumulated traveling had caught up with him but the concert didn't meet Sting's expectations: "It wasn't exactly your real audience. You had to write in for tickets so only the most *efficient* people got them. We went on stage to polite applause and I almost walked off. It could have been good. It *should* have been good."

It had been over a year since the Police had been in the studio. That summer had been set aside for writing and recording their third album. Only one new song 'Driven To Tears', had been brought into the band's live performance since 'Regatta De Blanc'. Sting had written it "as a reaction to watching the Third World die on the television every night. You know, reading a color supplement over a cup of coffee on Sunday morning and seeing a picture of a child well on the way to a horrible death." Oddly, this theme arose before he'd seen the reality.

Sting needed time off to write more songs and he retreated to his new house in Eire for two months to do just that. "I'd realized that I can't tour and write at the same time," he says. "I hadn't written a song in six months and I took my phone off the hook, didn't see anyone apart from Frances and Joseph, and wrote the songs that turned up on 'Zenyatta Mondatta'."

The move to Eire wasn't entirely voluntary. Both Sting and Andy had been advised by accountants that they should be 'non-resident' in England for the next year to avoid a huge tax bill.

New York Madison Square Gardens, 1981. Stewart: Basically America is a boring place and American people I don't give a damn about really . . . Anyway it's a lousy place musically and destitute culturally. But I am *very* American. I'm loud and obnoxious and I believe that you get what you deserve and work for — which is the basic American way of thinking."

Stewart ironically didn't have to leave England because he's an American citizen. He used the time before recording 'Zenyatta' to help his old associate Klark Kent who had 're-materialized' and wanted to make a record. Explaining to sceptics why Klark had to be completely alone in the studio and not use other musicians, Stewart said: "His relationship with other musicians is dominated by the fact that his physiology responds to his accentuated artistic output. His body chemistry is thereby affected in an unnatural way. The stench that comes off him makes it very difficult for him to work in a close confined atmosphere with other musicians. It also requires that the engineer wears lead underwear."

And to one doubting Thomas who suggested that Klark Kent was more like Stewart than Stewart was, he replied: "You've touched on something there. The point is that Klark Kent is more like everybody than anybody is!" Ten inches of Klark Kent appeared in vinyl form during June.

A&M had wanted a new Police record for the summer but as the 'Zenyatta' album wasn't going to be started until July they were stuck. To fill the gap they decided to release a package of the band's five singles thus far plus a sixth with a new version of 'The Bed's Too Big Without You' recorded for DJ Kenny Everett's British TV series and a live version of 'Truth Hits Everybody' recorded in Boston. The singles were pressed in blue vinyl and contained in a plastic folder.

When the six-pack was released at the end of May as a 'limited edition' of 58,000 at £5.99 it ran into critical flak. For three of the singles it was their third appearance and

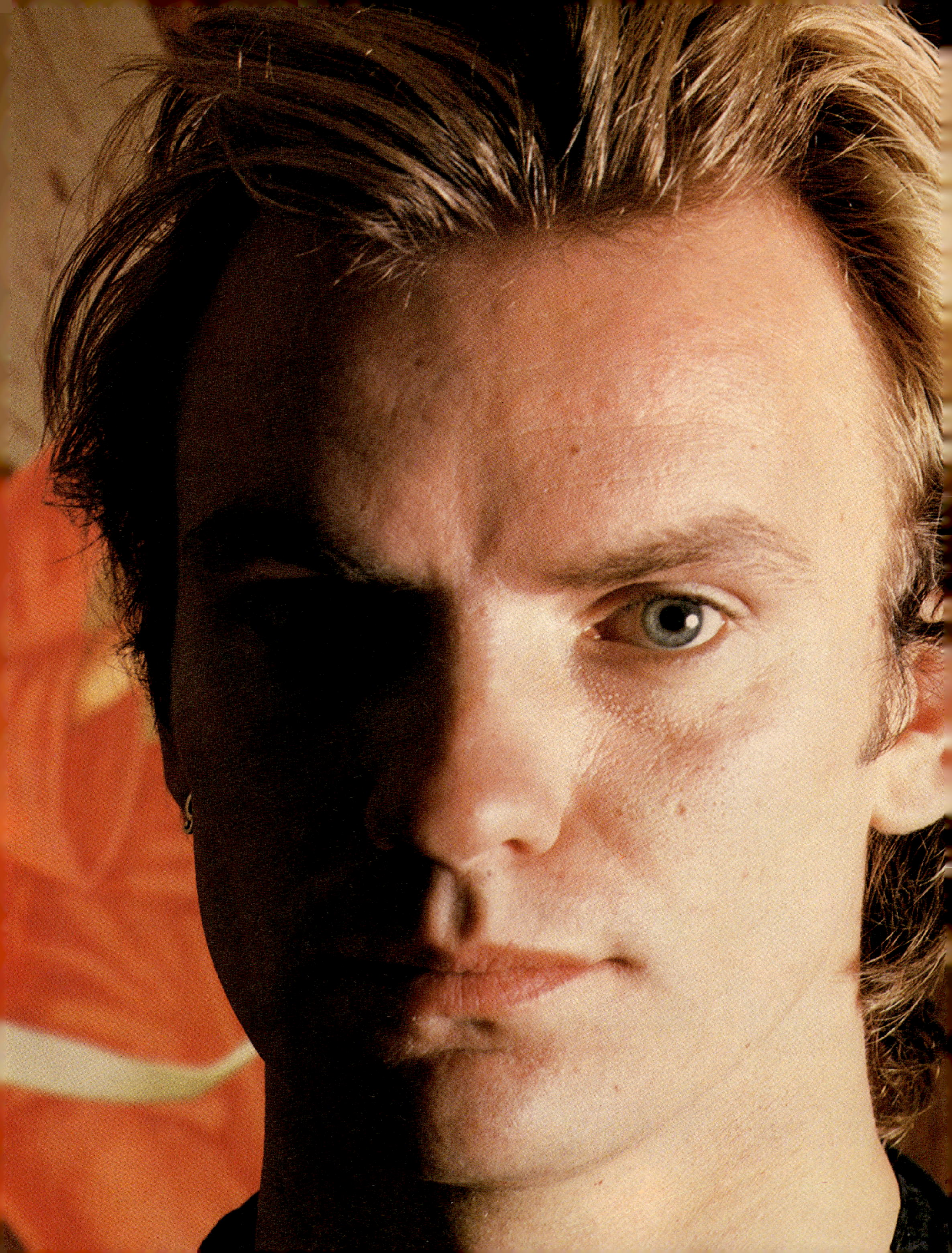

the band's most faithful fans were having to shell out for five singles that they already had in order to collect one that they hadn't. The band themselves weren't too happy about the idea. Stewart says: "It was a big mistake. The last thing we needed was another release of 'Roxanne'. It was a drag that there wasn't something new to suck people in to. We should have vetoed it but we were a long way away from Britain when the idea first came up."

It looked like a case of the band losing control over their output but Miles defends the move: "It *had* been discussed. There was a screaming match and then everyone forgot about it. The fact of the matter was that we had no product out. We had all these singles there. We wanted to make a really nice package at a really cheap price. I tell you, it's worth £50 now." Maybe, but it remains an unfortunate example of the Police being drawn into dubious commercial ploys.

The Police started recording 'Zenyatta' in July. For tax reasons they couldn't go back to Surrey Sound or any other British studio so they gathered up Nigel Gray and went over to Wisseloord in Holland.

That wasn't the only change. Before 'Regatta' they'd been hopefuls, now they were superstars. Not only that, they'd done it in an industry that was suffering a severe economic recession. A&M were banking on them, in every sense. The group themselves were well aware that they had a reputation to maintain. On top of that, while in Australia they'd agreed to play two large UK open air festivals — at Milton Keynes and Leixlip Castle — right in the middle of an already tight recording schedule.

No wonder Stewart says: "What was once a challenge became a responsibility. 'Zenyatta' should have been a lot better. The songs are good and we had more material which could have been good too. But the time factor screwed it all up. We had just bitten off more than we could chew.

"We had to take a week off to rehearse for the festivals. Then I remember arguing with Miles because he was going to start a Belgian tour earlier than planned. In fact it was only me screaming at Miles that got the dates canceled. As it was, we finished the album at 4am on the day we were supposed to start our next world tour. We went to bed for a few hours and then traveled down to Belgium for the first gig. It was cutting it very fine."

Sting felt much the same way: "I was keen to record 'Zenyatta' because I'd written a lot of songs for it, but when it came to going back on the road I had to be virtually dragged out of the house."

Andy recalls that it took the band a while to settle in the studio. "We were tired before we started because we'd worked for so long. The first week we were just doing backing tracks. They weren't really songs then. I remember listening to them and it seemed as if we hadn't really done anything. I felt a bit disoriented."

Nigel Gray believes the band didn't have enough good material when they started: "For 'Outlandos' they had a lot of songs that Sting had written and which they'd been playing on stage. For 'Regatta' Sting could delve back into his past to get more songs they could adapt. But by 'Zenyatta' the only material they had was what they'd been able to write in their month off.

"'Zenyatta' was quite experimental in many ways. Almost off the wall. The two singles were quite close to

Stewart: "The trouble with limos is everyone wants to pile in and by the time all the seats are taken, there's two people on the floor and one on your lap and you want to say 'Hey, I'll get out and catch the bus'."

Sting's original demos, but others were quite different. On 'Voices Inside My Head' I had to struggle to get them to do it the way they did, but right up to the last moment there was a possibility they'd use the original demo which just wasn't the Police. But we put some echo effects on the backing track and it became a disco hit in America! 'Shadows In The Rain' changed too. Originally that was a swinging little tune and really corny. I told Sting it was a pile of shit. But when we ran out of songs I told them to 'Policify' it and they did immediately. That's what they're so good at."

'Policification'? If it exists, Andy's the expert: "With 'When The World Is Running Down' Sting's demos sounded more like Sly And The Family Stone than the Police. But Stewart and I liked it and we started playing around with it. Finally, I changed the chords, put them through my pedal board and it started to sound like the Police."

Andy now had one more toy to add to his collection: "After Sting had put the vocals on 'Don't Stand So Close To Me' we looked for something to lift the middle of the song. I came up with a guitar synthesizer. It was the first time we'd used it. I felt it worked really well."

Nigel's role had grown too. "They leaned on me more heavily than before," he says. "If they came to an impasse they'd say 'Go on Nigel, produce us'. When they gave me the credit as producer on 'Regatta' and 'Zenyatta' I was pleased they'd recognized it.

"There was a problem with the studio in Holland though. Everything sounded enormous, but when I took the tapes back to England they sounded woolly and boring. It was very deceptive. So we had to remix the album. By then we'd run out of time and we landed up mixing five tracks in five hours which was crazy."

Nigel also had an argument with Miles over payment for 'Zenyatta': "I felt that my contribution to the first two albums which I'd done for a straight fee had been significant and I was owed a percentage point on 'Zenyatta'. It was a matter of honor really. But when my manager approached Miles to get a letter of agreement Miles went berserk. He said things like 'That's a hundred grand! Give him ten grand. He'll be famous, it will make his reputation'. Which was the truth of course. If they'd said 'Do it for nothing' I would have because any producer would jump at the chance of doing the Police.

"So eventually Miles, who's on a quarter of everything the band earn, told the band 'You can give him three-quarters of a point out of your royalties'. The band agreed, but I felt that was absurd. If the band didn't have the guts to stand up and say 'Look, we owe the guy a point, give it to him', then I wasn't interested. In the end I said 'Give me £25,000 and we'll continue negotiations later'. So they did, but it was clear that I wasn't going to get any more." Even including Nigel's fee, 'Zenyatta' cost only £35,000, still very cheap for a guaranteed million seller.

The two festivals at Milton Keynes and Leixlip Castle in July may have been an inconvenience to their recording plans, but the youth organizations who got musical equipment out of the Police's fees for the gigs would disagree. Charity didn't extend as far as any photographers who were intending to snap Sting using his upright bass for the first time on stage (he calls it Brian if you really want to know). They were asked to sign a three-page contract demanding 50 per cent of any syndication rights. Most of them ignored it and kept shooting.

At Leixlip Castle the Police had the rare experience of being targets for bottle throwers and Stewart was cut. Only Andy derived much pleasure from the gig. He ran into old flame Jenny Fabian who'd immortalized him in the book *Groupie* more than a decade earlier.

Back on the world tour after finishing 'Zenyatta', they filmed a French gig for a rock film called *Urgh – A Music War* which eventually came out in the middle of 1981. At another French gig Stewart was taken ill with food poisoning 20 minutes beforehand and his drum roadie Jeff Seitz had to take over. "He did a good job," remembers road manager Kim Turner. "He knew all Stewart's licks and he kept his head down so half the audience never noticed."

In Britain, 'Don't Stand So Close To Me' came out in mid-September and sold half a million copies in its first week of release. 'Zenyatta Mondatta' followed a couple of weeks later and gave them another double Number One. But, if the group had cause to feel complacent, Sting had a close view of what it's like when the boot's on the other foot when he went to see Frances play her most important role so far as Lady Macbeth in an Old Vic production starring Peter O'Toole. O'Toole was savaged by the critics with a venom that hadn't been seen for years although Frances was exempted from most of the onslaught.

The Police spent most of the rest of the year persuading the Americans that they were now lagging behind the rest of the world in terms of Police appreciation. The venues were getting bigger every time and the Americans certainly took to 'Zenyatta' with more gusto than they'd shown 'Regatta'. By the end of the year 'Zenyatta' was in the Top Ten and 'De Do Do Do De Da Da Da' was their first hit single there since 'Roxanne'.

Ian Copeland's FBI agency was now established and successful and Miles had set up his own record company in Los Angeles called International Record Syndicate, IRS (which gets some fascinating misdirected mail to the Internal Revenue Service). It was his direct answer to the American major record companies' continued lack of interest in the new wave. He signed several British and American acts such as the Stranglers, Sector 27, Magazine and Oingo Boingo who had previously been neglected.

At the end of that tour the Police turned south to Argentina for three concerts. They didn't mean much more there than they had in India but the potential was more immediate as Miles explains: "Before we went nobody had heard of the Police. Now I'm getting offers of 50,000 dollars to go back. It's good for the guys too. Sting wrote a great song over there influenced by Latin-American music. These inputs keep them fresh and it creates a glamor."

Glamor is not a word the Police would use to describe the concerts in Argentina however. "We were surrounded by police with machine guns goosestepping in front of the stage," says Sting. "Every time anyone showed any expression of joy or emotion they were flattened with a rifle butt. There was this girl in front of Andy and they got hold of her really roughly and started to drag her away. He wanted to stop them but as he was playing all he could do was stick out a foot and wave it at them. That's all he did.

"But the audience went berserk. They all rushed forward as if they'd been waiting for one spark. The riot police had their guns out and surrounded the theater. We were still playing and my roadie came up to me and said 'For God's sake don't insult them any more, they're going to arrest Andy'. Between songs I was getting these messages – 'Six months in prison at least'. And all the time I was trying to entertain the crowd, to channel that frenzy.

"Afterwards the promoter found a lawyer for us. He said 'You have to go down on this guy, crawl, nip it in the bud'. Then the police came in with guns and this big heavy guy who looked like Garcia of *Zorro*. He was a real pig of a man. It was him who'd been bullying this girl. He stood there with no expression on his face and Andy went up and apologized through interpreters in the most obsequious fashion he could muster. I just stood there remembering Egypt and thinking 'I couldn't do it, I couldn't do it'."

At Christmas the band came home and played three quick shows including a couple in a 5,000 capacity tent on Tooting Common in South London which was justly criticized for overcrowding. But finding the right venue that could hold even a proportion of the fans who wanted to see them in England was now a problem, particularly at short notice.

Christmas was even less of a pause than it had been the previous year and early in January they were back in America for The Big One – a sell-out concert at New York's Madison Square Garden, probably the most prestigious venue in the world. For Miles there was a special significance in being the first new wave band to play there: "We'd been first all along. A&M were telling us to wait but I said 'No'. And now we've done it we'll do two nights next time. The Cars did play there before but I never thought they were part of the new wave. They can't have been otherwise we wouldn't have been the first new wave band to play there!" There's no logic like Copeland logic.

The Police had fixed tours of Japan, Australia and Europe to follow, repeating what they'd done almost exactly a year earlier but missing out the exotic locations and concentrating on the major record markets. They'd even done Spanish and Japanese versions of 'De Do Do Do'. "Sting came in and did the vocals in Miami while I was working there," says Nigel Gray.

Sting's daily fitness regime includes running three miles, doing 60 sit-ups and 50 press-ups.

"We had a Spanish guy to tell us if it sounded right and we had a demo of someone singing the words in Japanese so we used that as a rough guide."

But that was probably Nigel's last involvement with the Police. "I'm not likely to be doing the next album. The fact that 'Zenyatta' had its problems and they weren't all that happy with it has given ammunition to the argument that they were right not to pay me the point I'd asked for.

"After we'd finished 'Zenyatta' and I'd come back and realized the mixes weren't as good as we thought they were, I told a roadie who was bringing my car back from Holland to bring the master tapes over with him. But when he passed through customs they stopped him and first of all they found all these porno magazines in the boot among everything we'd chucked in after the session. So then they found the tapes and confiscated them. A&M absolutely freaked and got their lawyers into action because the album was already late and they had to pay £12,000 to get the tapes back."

Sting says he'd like another producer: "I think it would do us good. It would have to be someone strong-willed who could challenge us. He'd probably have to be an established name himself. We need a new sparring partner. As soon as you stop fighting you stop caring."

But most of all they needed a break. They needed to stop being 'the Police' and discover themselves as individuals once more. The energy that had carried them from obscurity to international superstardom in less than two years was running low. The depression that frequently follows elation showed. In March 1981 they canceled the European portion of their tour and came home.

"We've been almost superhuman in the amount of work we've done," says Andy. "I don't think many people could have got through it, and that's not bragging." Sting agrees wholeheartedly: "We're all workaholics but I've realized this is as far as you can push a group in one go. We need a break from the pressures – mental, personal, fatigue in every form. I need it more than the others I think."

Stewart sees it strategically: "We can already detect a feeling that we've said all there is to be said for now. We haven't really got anything to do as a group so we might as well do nothing. We've used up our ammunition for the time being."

Films figure in the plans for each of the band although when they started their break none of them had made firm commitments. Sting had five offers on the go and had already turned down nearly as many more. But he'd gone straight into a leading role in a British TV play *Artemis 81*. Andy had a film offer too and Stewart was at large with his camera muttering about a TV project.

They had their separate musical ideas to follow as well. Sting had started writing songs for other performers such as Grace Jones and recorded a version of Bob Dylan's 'I Shall Be Released' for a TV film soundtrack. Andy had plans for an album "very different from the Police" and Stewart was going to concentrate on songwriting unless distracted by Klark Kent.

As Sting says: "This is the end of a chapter."

8
WALKING ROUND THE ROOM

"I suppose you've heard the one about them supporting the record industry of Great Britain," says Nick Jones in a sardonic moment. Indeed.

Sting says: "I support the record industry of Great Britain. The Police is the only act that pays. It's true! Everybody else is just flim-flam supported by decomposing record companies." This is an exaggeration – but only just.

He laughs about it. He's pleased and proud. On the other hand being the hope of the team does produce enormous pressure, probably more so on Sting than the other members of the band because he has to produce the raw material: songs.

As Stewart relates: "There's one immediate way of getting yourself fired from A&M, the ultimate no-no. You go up to Sting and say 'Written any good tunes lately?' "

Of course, tunes have been flowing out of Sting since he was in short trousers. But their function has changed. Now they have to entertain millions, producing huge profits and employment in every sphere touched by the rock business – not just record companies but pressing plants, sleeve and label printers and designers, badge and T-shirt makers, journalism, publishing, printing, newsagents, TV and radio. And authors.

That's what Sting has to put behind him when he settles down to write. "If you're trying to be creative, trying to be original, you can't come up with a brilliant idea every day. It just doesn't happen," he says. "I used to go through months and months of paranoia about it, but the more you worry about it the worse it gets."

It's during these blocks that the conflict of emotions about his special place within the band reaches an acute pitch: "I know for a fact when we're approaching an album Stewart and Andy are thinking 'We'll write a few songs okay, but Sting will write the album'. And I know I've got to do it, but is it there? I do resent that ... even though there'd be terrible trouble if they did suddenly come up with the best songs, just hell!

"And I'm sure if I saw the potential in one of their compositions as a single I'd accept it. The thing is once the hit is written I believe it doesn't belong to me any more and stands on its own two feet. I haven't felt that with anything of Andy's or Stewart's yet though, and after all it's me who has to sing the fucker."

The potential threat to group harmony is obvious. What has kept friction on this score to a manageable minimum is that the cool self-criticism of Andy and Stewart is completely in line with Sting's. In retrospect they know they haven't cut it yet.

There's an almost mystic quality about the build-up of tension as they approach The Time. Stewart says: "Sting is aware that if he plays me one of his demos before The Time I'll only be disparaging about it. We have to be absolutely ready." He adds laconically: "Sting does actually like some of my stuff." 'Bombs Away' on 'Zenyatta', a typical Copeland observation of Third World politics, is quite funny and effective because Sting's offhand vocal is exactly right for the subject of a fat dictator carelessly disposing of the lives of thousands.

Stewart feels comfortable enough with such consolations. He's not so sure about Andy though: "Andy has to really struggle to get his material noticed. I'm usually ready to work on it with him, but it's not so easy with Sting. He'll try it all right. There's an expression of anguish on his face though. A 'What are we wasting our time on this for?' look." Or as Nigel Gray puts it: "Sting won't *identify* with Andy's songs."

Sting would probably agree: "Andy isn't a writer of melodies. It's very separate from musicianship and it's very hard for a marvelous technical musician to take. I mean I'm not a great musician, but I do rate myself as a songwriter."

Fortunately Andy can rationalize it: "I suppose it's a little frustrating in a way, but I don't think I can write pop songs like Sting because I'm not vocally equipped. He opens his mouth and that golden voice comes out whereas Stewart and I just croak away. It's not a source of pain. Or rather it *was* something to deal with and I think I've sorted it out. I don't feel insecure about it."

The matter of artistic fulfilment can be continually resolved by sheer common sense, but cash might have become a more bitter pill. With the Police established as a hit machine, Sting as writer has only to pull the lever and out comes a jackpot of publishing royalties. However, from the outset they agreed to share all publishing under

81

a deal which apparently gives the writer half of the proceeds and the other two a quarter each as 'arrangers'.

This recognizes that in one area of their music the Police *are* unequal. Sting is an inspired songwriter and the band value it like a sculptor values the finest marble. "Songs, that's what the group's about," says Andy, sweeping his own virtuosity aside without a qualm.

Even Sting, the Face, wants to vanish behind his handiwork: "We're selling the song, not technical ability. That has to be hidden for the sake of expression. The essence is the words and the tune. I've written songs that are very powerful and when we're on stage I want to say 'Right, I'll leave you to it' and let the audience take it. If it's going without me I will stop playing. The best thing you can do is *not* play."

Community singing may not be the critics' idea of a rock concert, but Police audiences seem to approve. Sting says: "It's a lovely thing. It's beautiful. We need more of it. The tendency in society is to become more and more alienated. Put the headphones on and blot out the sound of the street. There'll be video sunglasses next. We need . . . touch. That's why India was so strong for me. They have no choice, they're overcrowded, they have to be seven people to a room, they have to touch."

Trying to explain the creative process which leads to 20,000 people roaring 'Roxanne' together isn't easy, but Sting has analyzed the mystery to an extent: "I find if I've got a title I can write a song. It's the hook. Usually it happens unconsciously when I'm not thinking, half-asleep, half-awake. If I'm lying in bed in the morning and one of those key phrases comes to me, I get up and run down to my guitar before I lose it. It's amazing! It's a mistake to think of artists as so inspired, so God-given-talented, that they just start at the beginning with a brilliant first line and rattle through in perfect sequence."

The magic phrase sometimes comes unexpectedly to start a whole new train of thought and sometimes crystalizes an idea he's been chewing over for ages – like 'Don't Stand So Close To Me': "I wanted to write a song about sexuality in the classroom. I'd done teaching practice at secondary schools and been through the business of having 15-year-old girls really fancying me – and me really fancying them! How I kept my hands off them I don't know . . .

"Then there was my love for *Lolita* which I think is a brilliant novel. But I was looking for the key for eighteen months and suddenly there it was. That opened the gates and out it came: the teacher, the open page, the virgin, the rape in the car, getting the sack, Nabokov, all that."

'Walking On The Moon' came about through the opposite process: "I was drunk in a hotel room in Munich, slumped on the bed with the whirling pit when this riff came into my head. I got up and started walking round the room singing 'Walking round the room, ya ya, walking round the room'. That was all. In the cool light of morning I remembered what had happened and I wrote the riff down. But 'Walking Round The Room' was a stupid title so I thought of something even more stupid which was 'Walking On The Moon'."

One daft, accidental line became a perfect pop image, grand and simple. Floating on that airy spacious arrangement you might take the astronaut image literally for the first two lines: *'Giant steps are what you take, walking on the moon/I hope my legs don't break, walking on the moon'*. Then it declares itself as a love song: *'We could walk forever . . . We could live together . . .'*

Everyone knows the feeling and yet nobody had said it quite like that before. *'Walking back from your house, walking on the moon.'* That's the story. Young love for sure, but not made soft and silly by some aging hack out to 'exploit a market'. That low-gravity, high-stepping sensation of ecstasy, the niggling fear that you might come a cropper, the bashful hopes that it could be permanent, the pervasive dreamlike quality: it's as if Sting

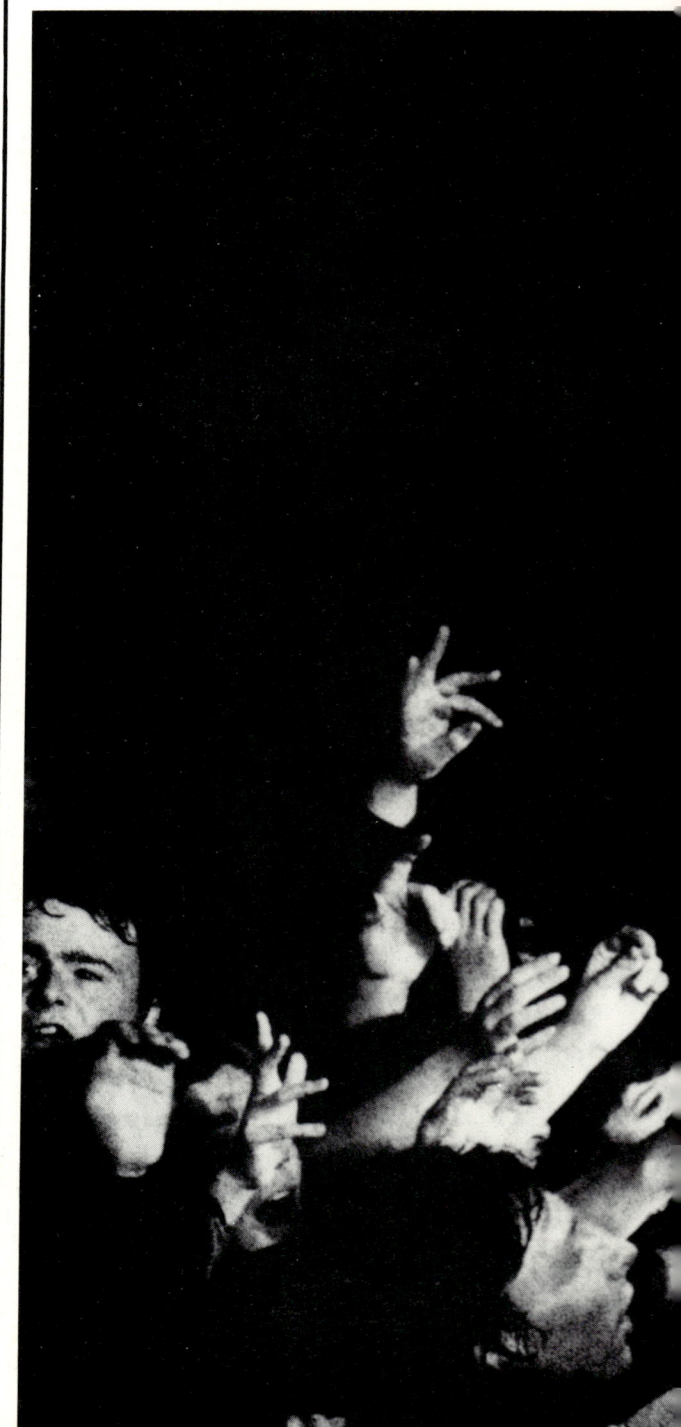

Sting: "If you can transcend the screaming you can take a generation with you into something else. It's a real challenge."

didn't just 'understand', but was sharing his own emotions.

It seems that most of Sting's songs have come from looking inside himself. But, there are occasions when being alert to other people will give him what he needs. 'Shadows In The Rain', the most adventurous and enigmatic track on 'Zenyatta', was originally stirred by John Scott, former bassist with Alberto Y Lost Trios Paranoias who the Police toured with in late '78: "That's got a great opening line, *Woke up in my clothes again this morning*'. John, who was a complete madman and loony, used to appear in the morning and say things like 'Slept in my clothes again last night'. That led me to *'Don't know exactly where I am'* and so on".

'De Do Do Do', which turned out to be probably the Police's most misinterpreted song, was to a degree the Catholic Sting in the confessional: "I wanted to write about the perversity of words, their dangers. Of course it was a self-indictment too. I'm ... clever with words". Most critics rounded on him for descending to nursery rhyme level to score a hit.

Sting was baffled and hurt, but his 'cleverness' had tied a noose round his own neck: *'Don't think me unkind/Words are hard to find/They're only cheques I've left unsigned/From the banks of chaos in my mind/And when their eloquence escapes me/Their logic ties me up and rapes me'*.

Anybody's life, including his own, is grist to the creative mill: "Look, the whole thing about being a writer is that with every traumatic experience part of you is thinking 'I

Sting: "I've used cocaine to get me on stage when nothing else would... I think that is a justifiable use of a chemical."

can *use* this'. I've had bad times in my life. Loneliness hits me a lot. And I glorify in it! Without it I wouldn't have written 'So Lonely' or 'Message In A Bottle' or 'The Bed's Too Big Without You'. I thank God for the times I was down, the time my girlfriend left me, the time my girlfriend committed suicide, the awful reactionary school I went to which I fought so hard. I'm praying for something to fight against now...

"This is scary. Do you know I even cynically think about the day that Frances and I might break up. I love her dearly, I mean I'm devoted to her and yet I can see how useful alienation is. If you're determined to be an artist you have to be hungry and my life now is too easy. I'm full. The artist in me is looking for death, for destruction. Artists are perverse. They're not normal. They ain't. I'm not normal."

He has observed a development in his writing: "The songs on 'Outlandos' are all me, me, me. '*I feel so lonely*'. Roxanne, *I won't share you with another boy*', '*I was born in the 50s*'. With 'Zenyatta' I think I've stopped writing about me and turned to what's happening outside. I couldn't have written 'Driven To Tears' or 'When The World Is Running Down' three years ago. I hadn't seen the world for a start. And I was too interested in me."

Creating a song is a solitary labor. But playing it is quite different. The band must open up to one another totally so that they can give everything, even the stuff they didn't know they had.

Andy Summers has the crucial role. Stewart is the founder of the band without whom etc. Sting is the writer/voice/Face without whom etc. Andy is the other fella. He lives by musicianship alone. Stewart enthuses about him: "Andy's most important feature as a guitarist is his ability to play anything. There's no chord that he can't arrive at. Sting or I will say 'How about something like this?' and sing it at him and he'll play it back straight away."

'Lubrication' is the quality Sting appreciates most in Andy: "We need someone easy-going in the group. With another Stewart Copeland or another Sting we wouldn't have lasted this long, we would definitely have gone overboard."

But Andy is harder than that in Stewart's view: "He's not a mild personality at all. He's very strong and fiery. You could snidely say that the Police happened just in time for him. On the other hand the Police wouldn't have happened without him, without all the experience he's picked up from zillions of gigs, we wouldn't have taken the good decisions that we did."

Soundman Kim Turner admires Andy's mastery of the guitar and special effects: "A song which sounds pretty bland when Sting brings in the demo can be turned into magic by Andy's guitar. He produces his whole sound himself. People think I put on a lot of the effects live, but it's all Andy."

If Andy's whole case is musicianship, his learned friends occasionally have to take the side of the prosecution too. Stewart says: "Sometimes I think that too many sessions can sterilize the talent. Inspiration can get lost. For instance, you'll hit a problem and say 'I can't think of anything to go here. You got any ideas?'. And he'll go 'Weedly, weedly, wee' — the Guitar Solo, a piece of pure Eric Clapton. He has a huge wardrobe of licks and the first ones he'll whip out will usually be the wrong ones.

"Most of the guitar you hear Andy play he's probably thought of himself, but only after we've spent hours saying 'No!' and making suggestions like 'Why doncha

"Somebody should clip Sting round the head and tell him to stop singing in that ridiculous Jamaican accent. They make great records, they can all play, they're all pretty and I can't stand them." Elvis Costello.

take off all the strings and then see what you can do?'. The archetypal Police guitar solo is on 'When The World Is Running Down' (*he imitates a motor bike whining past*) and that started out as 'Weedly, weedly, wee'."

Perhaps Andy's difficulty is that he is the eternal student caught in the professor's chair, as his old friend Zoot Money suggests: "It's easy while you're faceless. Now he is being observed whereas what he wants to do is observe other people".

Joining a band where the 'guitar hero' was outlawed caused teething problems for Andy. "Like most guitarists I wanted to play solos, flash off a bit. There's a certain amount of insecurity and penis thrusting involved," he says with an impish smile. "But the change hasn't bothered me. My reputation as a guitarist certainly hasn't suffered because of it. I suppose it could seem as if I'm a fragmented musical personality, a chameleon, but it's not so."

The guitar solo on 'Driven To Tears' illustrates the sort of continuous wrestling match which goes on beneath the stylish surface of their music and the way the principal actors' memories of stressful events can vary wildly. Sting says that he was fuming when they recorded it: "What you hear on 'Zenyatta' sounds very anarchic. It took about three hours to do and I wouldn't let Andy out of the studio until he got it. I put him in a really bad mood. 'Look, this has got to destroy all guitar solos! Atonal! Just fuckin' play like you hate me!' Then it was great. Everything about it is wrong and it's perfect".

But Andy recollects: "On 'Driven To Tears' I went straight into the studio and played virtually the solo that's on the record straight off. Sting really responded to it and said 'Yeah, let's have more of that!' so I did three or four variations and we kept the best one". Take your pick!

Stewart's special status as founding father of the band doesn't protect him from whatever aggro is going. Superficially he seems a hard person to put down. Ask him to discuss his own ability and he'll spill self-confidence over you like a volcano spilling lava. "When I look around at the competition — I find there isn't any!" he'll holler.

The thing is, with a pinch of salt added, his claims aren't far-fetched in his chosen field of regatta de blanc. Andy gladly offers endorsement: "You only have to hear about how many drummers rave about him. Rhythmically he's invented a lot of stuff and people are copying him all over the place. He's improved tremendously since '77.

"The first time I played with him I didn't like his drumming because he seemed to be all over the place, incredibly rushed because of the punk thing. The irony with Stewart is that he likes fast, heavy rock, but what he's really good at is our medium-tempo reggae stuff. For the Police he's brilliant, amazingly rhythmic, these jungly little licks. On 'Message In A Bottle' he's superb."

'Message' is Stewart's own favorite showcase, though some people prefer his work on 'The Bed's Too Big Without You'.

Nigel Gray amplifies the plaudits: "He knows how to pick a rhythm that will really make a track move. His drum part will be a third as intricate as someone else would play and yet he'll create a much better feel".

On the other hand turn to Sting and you find the praise and blame erupting in one outburst because in the intimate partnership of bass and drums the good and the bad are opposite sides of the same coin. Stewart has so much drive, it's dynamic, inspiring, and yet "That energy of Stewart's behind you all the time has to be controlled. 'Wait! Wait!' He *explodes* with it.

"On stage he's not that responsible a performer that

he knows exactly what he's doing. It's great *and* it's a drawback. He gives everything too much and too often. It's the drummer's problem. They're all mad. Anyway, it comes back to rivalry between me and Stewart. He's at the back and he wants to be at the front. What's so fascinating about him is he's a lead guitarist in the guise of a drummer. And of course I'm a lead guitarist with a bass.

"So when Stewart's good he's great and when he's bad he's fuckin' awful. The best drummers are orchestral. They play the song without losing the pulse. That's what I need from him, the pulse, not the flash."

There's no doubt that Stewart is sometimes like a poet laureate who can't quite remember his ABC. Nigel Gray says "His biggest fault is time-keeping" and Andy agrees with Sting that "You often want him to play less, relax a bit and just lay it down."

But one of Stewart's strengths is his awareness of the technical blemishes he still hasn't corrected: "Yeah, sometimes I'm not precise enough. I listen to tracks on 'Zenyatta' and hear spaces where I'm not right on the nail.

"Thinking back to my Curved Air days, I didn't have any discipline — I had all the technique and I couldn't hold a steady beat. I hadn't realized that I had a function to fulfil as well as an ego to exhibit. But you can't be an upfront drummer. Sting's voice and songs make the Police what it is. I know I'm red-hot and all that, but the Police would probably have been pretty successful with some drummer who could *just* hold the beat — like Talking Heads for example."

The ultimate difficulty may be that the Copeland bloodstream doesn't have a steady pulse. Stewart leaps through life in seven-league boots. Still, not too fast to learn: "There's an album by Donny Hathaway (*late American soul artist*) where the drummer does nothing but 'um *pa* um *pa* um *pa*' all the way through. I could listen to that all night. It turned me on to pulse. A lot of the time when I'm on my own I like to sit and play the drums like that, 'um *pa* um *pa* um *pa*', and it feels great, like riding a bicycle. I practise it almost as a meditation."

Criticizing Sting is something else altogether. At times Andy and Stewart's battles against his musical will must feel like having a conker fight with a wrecking ball. As Andy says: "It's hard to fault Sting. You can only talk about him in accolades. I love his voice. Technically it's very good too. Working with Eberhard Schoener I heard him sing some extraordinary stuff and he can imitate any style from blues to cabaret. He's excellent on bass too, very effective, not self-indulgent. I mean, he doesn't play like Stanley Clarke, he hasn't got that skill, but I think he's more musical."

Stewart can only agree: "As a singer there isn't anybody in the world who could do a better job than Sting. He's in tune and he's got a great rhythmic feel. He was born with that voice, but he uses it so well too. And I've got a definite telepathy with his bass playing."

Sting's voice is the one element of the Police which Nigel Gray can't 'produce': "There's nobody in the world can tell Sting how to sing. He records vocals first time after one run through. Wind the track back a couple of times for the harmonies and that's it. His voice is the best I've ever recorded, just the character of it. I remember mixing 'Don't Stand So Close To Me' in the studio early one morning in absolute ecstasy at the way the chorus voices build up. Not many bands really have a *singer* you

Stewart: "You could say that the Police happened just in time for Andy. On the other hand, the Police wouldn't have happened without him."

---

know. There's usually just someone who belts out the vocals."

What does Sting think of all this? Well, he doesn't deny it. But even Sting is human and he does err. With an air of aimiable relish Stewart says: "There is something I'll have to harrass him about. He used to have the most finely tuned ears in the group, but lately because he's switched to fretless bass some of the intonation has tended to get a bit screwy when we're playing live. One day I'm going to sneak in and put the frets back on!"

He'll have to elbow Andy aside first though: "The point has been raised more than once and Sting won't change. It's not that big an issue with me. I don't think the audiences pick up on the odd mistake very much. And the upright bass (*also fretless*) is certainly no gimmick. It's got a much stronger, bassier, more resonant sound and visually it's contributed to the image of the group. Sting is prepared to try things and he dives straight in, very bold. He's much more adventurous than I am in that respect. I'd be trying things out at a few soundchecks before I committed myself."

All right, musically Sting is a paragon. But he does have an 'artistic temperament' and an overpowering public persona which can be hard for Stewart and Andy to cope with. As Andy assesses it: "Sting knows his strengths and when he decides to turn on the power sometimes you have to ... deal with him."

Stewart has a word for it. Stingola. "It works like this. A journalist comes on the road with the band to write a feature. I talk to him for hours, Andy talks to him for hours and Sting never says a word — except that just once he walks through the room where I'm busy bending the guy's ear and he says 'Where's the toilet?'. *And that's the headline!*"

He collapses in laughter. But not necessarily on the day he opens the magazine and reads the story.

Sting makes no bones about having deliberately manipulated the media and in particular he set his sights on certain journalists such as Paul Morley of the New Musical Express who went to Bombay with the band: "I'd twigged that Paul was very influential on that paper — after he'd slagged off our first album. It was my job to get in there and win him over. When we did the interview he was really into my game, but he just went overboard." The front page, the centerspread and most of the words focussed on Sting.

"Andy and Stewart were furious. Livid. At me. They think I engineer all this publicity. I do in a way but ... I'm just doing my job. I'm the frontman off-stage as well as on. They have to put up with it. I've no sympathy with them when they get like that.

"It went on that way and got more and more frustrating so now it's arranged through our Press Agent that Andy and Stewart do almost all the talking. But then ... after a while *I* begin to feel ignored. 'Hey, this isn't right!' The problem gets worse and worse. We did a photo session with Alan Ballard for *The Sun* and he says 'Sting, could you come forward a bit?'. So I do. (*Fierce American tones*) 'I don't like this, we get too much of Sting out in

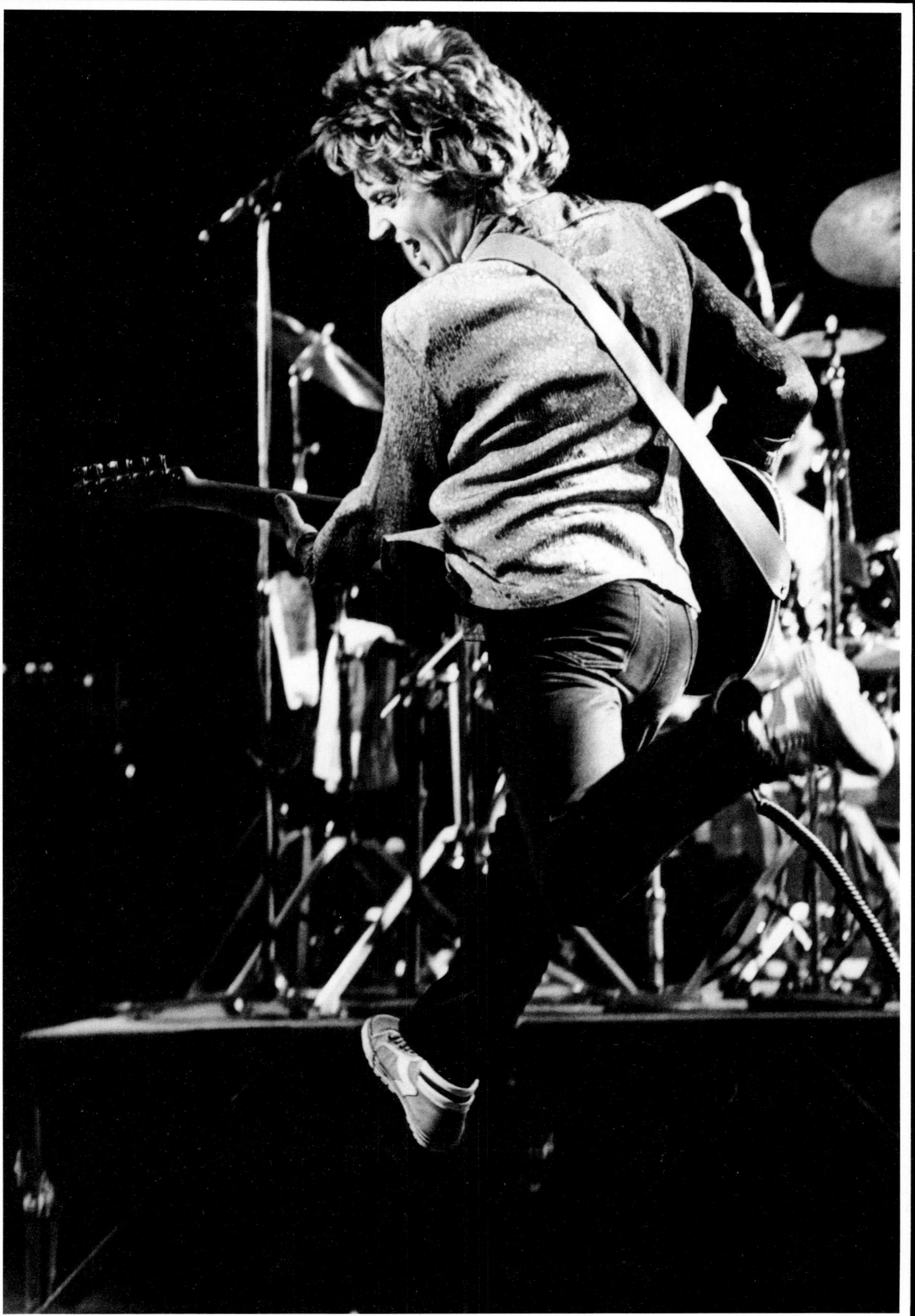

front.' So I stand humbly behind Stewart.

"I don't want to play that game. I can't stand the feeling that there's this jockeying for position going on. It's pathetic."

Stewart and Andy's problem is that professionally they are on display alongside a masterpiece. To Stewart it's a source of great amusement when he's not actually hopping mad about it: "I read a quote of mine somewhere – which is a quote in itself – saying 'I don't care if Sting is Superman. That doesn't make him better than me!'

"It's true he can be dangerous to be around. He has a tendency to eat people. Because he has such an incredibly high output of everything it takes. I mean, look at the guy. The talent, the voice, the intelligence, the personality, the looks. It all adds up and unless you have a high opinion of yourself it can be very trying on your self-esteem to work with him day after day.

"But it doesn't bother me. I have a lot of faith in my own talent although I recognize that it isn't the particular kind that gets your face on the front of magazines. I have my musical ability *and* my ability to enjoy myself. In some ways I'm probably better at that than Sting. I find it easier to smile than he does. I manage to keep my pecker up most of the time."

Happily whenever the media do knock him down the fans are there to pull him up again: "All right Sting is represented as the sex star, but my mail is all partisan. 'I hate Sting and I hate Andy and you're the one that's most handsome.' It's all ridiculous, I know it's got nothing to do with our music and they're only looking at the pictures saying 'Oo, that one's got a nice nose' and 'Oo, isn't he tall' – but actually I'm quite knocked out. So Sting made Number One in the *Smash Hits* magazine's Most Fanciable Person poll. Well I was fifth, I beat David Bowie and Bob Geldof, and that's not bad for a drummer!"

Sting may lead the media a dance, but he doesn't lead the band. The Face is not and cannot be The Boss. There's far too much at stake. Kim Turner, the inside outsider, observes: "It's never Sting's group. He would never be where he is without Andy and Stewart. I wouldn't ever want to see him try and dominate – even though the others wouldn't allow him to." Stewart affirms: "Sting didn't take my band off me. The Police is still my band and I'll carry on painting 'Police' on the walls until someone takes it off me."

The human geometry of the triangle holds them together. Andy is especially conscious of it: "Each one of us is out for himself and we've achieved so much because our three egos are all very strong. We have energy, ambition. And in a three-piece the roles are more dynamic. From experience I know that in quartets you tend to pair off. There's a tensile strength in a trio."

Very tense at times. Discussing their relationships with each other it emerges that they all think of themselves as peacemakers – and warriors!

Sting: "I fight tooth and nail for what I want. I'm very myopic about it. Stewart is a very similar character and there's a lot of conflict between us whereas Andy weaves his way through."

Stewart: "One of my standard roles in this band is keeping Sting off Andy's back. Sting can be very abusive and ride roughshod over people's sensibilities. I'm immune because I don't have any sensibilities. But Andy sometimes needs moral support from me."

Andy: "Sting often steps between Stewart and me. We have differences ... on most things. Whereas Sting and I tend to agree. In fact all the time it goes round in a circle."

Perhaps it adds up to friendship. Deeper than that even. Thinking it over one night Sting says "I have terrific rows with Stewart. On the other hand I can say to him 'I love you' and he's said the same to me. That's not usual between men who aren't homosexual I think. I wouldn't say the same to Andy though I'd probably seek out his company more and he is a very good friend."

Stewart responds, a little nonplussed: "Yeah. Mm ... There's a strong personal bond. We were friends to begin with, then that waned and became a professional relationship. But it's started to get much more intense ... You know, it's surprising how little I know about Sting. I'll have to read this book to find out. He doesn't usually talk about those things unless you're harrassing him and asking questions."

But would you ever have heard of the Police without Miles Copeland?

As the manager of the major new band of the early 80s he has played a large part in overturning traditional business thinking on a) high recording costs b) massive advances from record companies to groups c) access to America for unknown British groups d) establishing independent record labels in the States with national distribution.

Anyone who's met Miles has an opinion about him and probably an anecdote. If you could ignore him you could also overlook a passing tornado. Miles's own favorite views of himself are summed up by the Press cuttings he will sometimes quote: "One reporter said I was like 'an electrical engineer on speed'. *The Los Angeles Times* called me 'the Colonel Tom Parker of the new wave'. I love all that stuff." Parker was the late Elvis Presley's manager, a hundred per cent three-ring-circus showman. That's Miles's real frame of reference.

But listen to people who have worked with him over the years and showbiz glitter isn't what comes across: "He's not into hierarchy and he's not a materialist. He won't stand on ceremony about who does what. If he sees the bog's dirty he'll clean it"; "He often seems rude because he's got no small talk, not because he means to be abrupt"; "You'll find him talking a lot more about 'product' than about the people who work for him"; "Well I expect he's better than 85 per cent of the monsters who run record companies anyway."

Vermillion Sands, graphic designer at Faulty, says: "Talking to Miles is like talking to your father sometimes. He's like a warlord. You go to him for everything. You should have an argument with him. He has a tremendous sense of *rage*. I'm not saying he's a violent man, I've never seen him hit a human being, but he's certainly bust up some telephones."

"He who pays the piper breaks the phone," sighs Nick Jones.

Vermillion notices a startling contradiction between Miles and his father: "He's not secretive. He'll leave contracts lying about for all to see."

Sting sees an almost religious fervour in him: "If Miles had been born in the last century he would have been a Presbyterian minister. A hellfire and damnation

Sting: "I do not give myself easily."

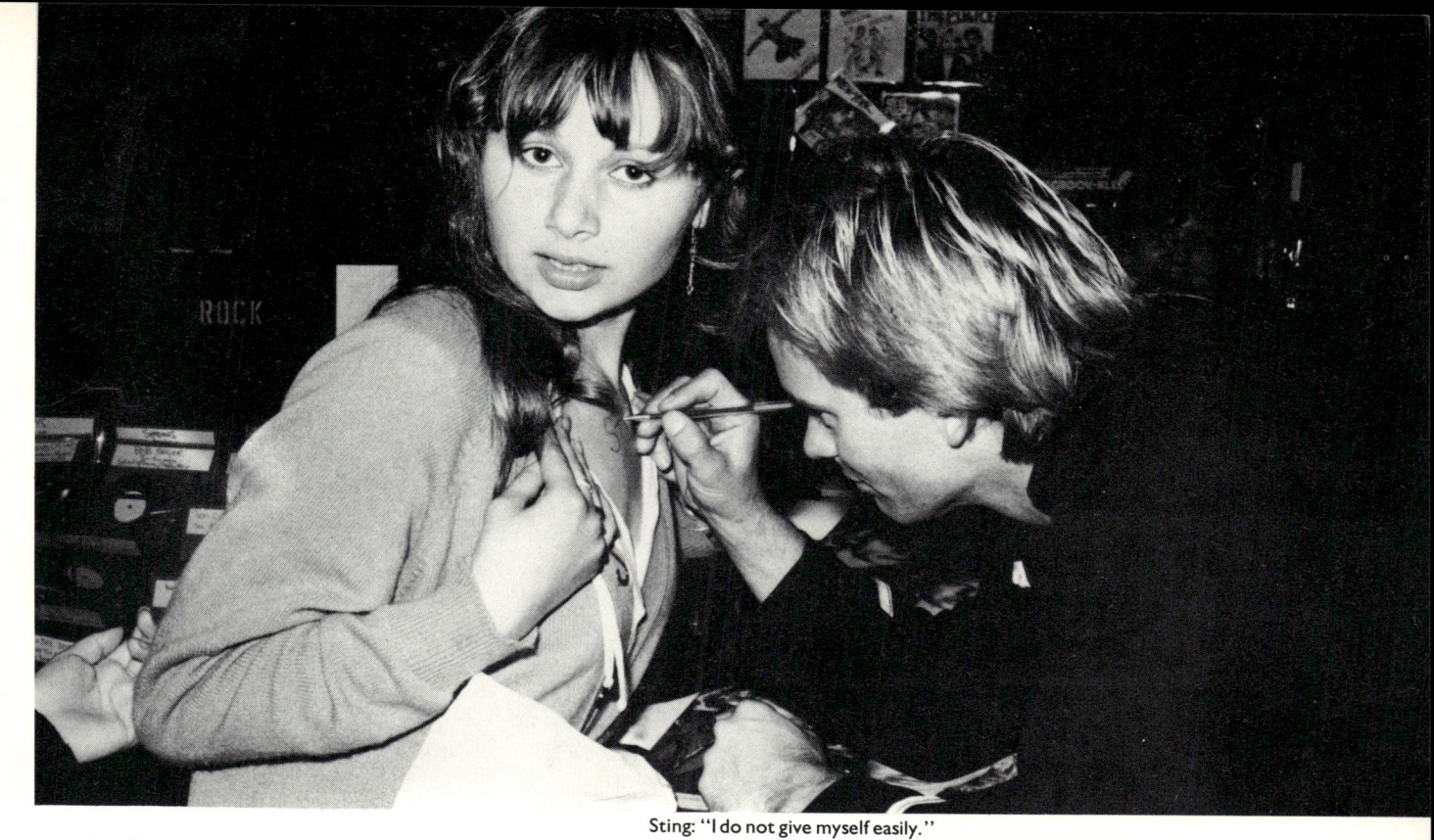

preacher." Miles would buy that on occasions. Laughing at himself – he can do that downhill with a following wind – he will proclaim that he is the "high priest" of new wave in America and admit that, playing that role, "I'm doctrinaire beyond the point of rationality."

Stewart is less convinced of his brother's spiritual side. He hands him compliments like exploding cigars: "Miles is a wonderful human being. Or rather he is wonderful, but I'm not sure he's a human being. He might be a robot dropped in by Strategic Air Command at the end of the war."

Certainly dealing with Miles must be like trying to hold a firecracker in the palms of your hands. But the crucial question for anyone working with a rock manager is 'Can I trust him?'. As a breed they have bad habits and an alarming reputation.

Nigel Gray, who had a run-in with Miles over money for 'Zenyatta Mondatta' says that Miles is "... so greedy. A good businessman fights for every penny, but there are certain people you shouldn't have to fight." Contrast that view of Miles on the ramparts with his magnanimity to Kim Turner back in '73 when he freed him from Cat Iron and kissed goodbye to £10,000 worth of investment without a tremor. The difference may be that he had accepted Kim as part of the team, whereas Nigel was an independent entrepreneur and, as such, competition.

Nick Jones recalls Miles paying John McLaughlin thousands of pounds about two years late when the guitarist had long since written it off to experience: "It blew his mind. Miles *is* basically honest." Stewart adds one of his complimentary backfires: "Yeah, Miles is honest. I don't mean he doesn't tell lies. Everyone in rock 'n' roll does that. But he doesn't steal."

Money is the tool of his trade and yet, by all accounts, Miles has no personal interest in it. Police film maker Derek Burbidge says: "Miles is the poorest millionaire I've ever met. He never has any money. Adding lots of noughts to a bank account doesn't interest him". Stewart confirms: "He doesn't drink, he doesn't smoke, he doesn't have a car and he's really puritan about drugs. He doesn't spend anything except on bands. That's his livelihood and his hobby. I try to persuade him to buy new clothes but he never does."

What does turn him on then? It has to be power/control. Being on top of a situation. Winning.

He lost once. His BTM empire of the early 70s went from prosperity to ruin within a couple of years. Miles says that collapse made him aware of a drastic error in his thinking: an accountant's approach to rock. "That was a serious business mistake," he says. That's why he has been so active in promoting the new wave as a whole since '77. Even where no direct profit accrued to his groups he felt that he was laying the foundations of a youth culture which would ultimately benefit him. Or, as preacher Miles puts it: "We had to take this generation and make it fulfil itself!"

The Police naturally rate him very highly. To say that it helps him to have a brother in the band would be an understatement, but Stewart understands Miles's faults and there's no question of him defending his conduct no matter what.

Stewart says: "Like any manager Miles has to be watched very carefully. The way to use him is to talk to him once a week, tell him what's happening, and he will advise you very shrewdly about the next move. He's good on overall strategy but bad on important details – like the time I needed my drumkit to do a TV show and found that he'd lent it to Gene October for a Chelsea gig."

Miles is well aware that the rapid expansion of the Police industry makes their affairs more messy and exposes some of his lack of precision: "The bigger anything gets the less together it gets in some ways. It's

Stewart: "I was a late developer in every respect. I was physically small for my age, bespectacled, utterly dreadful at my lessons, a real population statistic."

inevitable. The group is going to have to come to terms with that. So am I. If I was going to keep a 24-hour watch on the Police I'd have to hire another ten people and double my commission. The group aren't going to pay me any more so we have to face it.

"We've always been a bit schlocky. I'm not the kind of guy where every detail is watched, every penny squeezed out of the promoter. He makes an extra three or four hundred dollars, so what? The more he makes the more I make in the end. The important thing is that we get there."

But their choice not to employ those extra people means that some valuable work is neglected. The Police grouch about the way their UK fan club is run, yet Nick Jones argues that all would be well if they'd put some money into it. He recalls their objections to the club sending out photocards with their printed autographs, then not coming in to supply the signatures themselves.

Another matter for regret is that Miles's commitment to the independent label scene in the UK seems to have waned. By mid-'81, although he was still pushing the IRS energetically in the States, the Faulty labels in the UK were losing their identity and when IRS (UK) was formed it was licensed to A&M. Nick says: "Miles has injected vast sums of his own money into Faulty. But we've started to lose bands like the Fall who left us after two albums and four singles because of their ideological differences with the way Miles was going – and the fact that we were always short of money and didn't pay their royalties on time. Well, there were times when Miles's interest in the alternative scene was cursory. 'What do I need with ideals when I manage the biggest band in the world?'. You know."

Something did seem to have come sadly adrift when at Christmas, 1980, the Police's senior road crew got bonuses of up to £2,500 a man and the staff at Faulty got nothing, "not even a box of chocolates and a thankyou" as one disgruntled member said. None of this is quite in accord with Miles's view that the unknown and up-and-coming new bands are the foundations on which the edifice of the Police is built.

If Miles might accept some criticism that he does tend to spread himself too thinly he firmly denies the common allegation that he has pushed the Police too far and too fast: "There are four people keen on the band working hard. Stewart, Sting, Andy and me. Most artists say they want to be successful and a big star, but they don't really want it bad. Stewart and Sting want it *bad*. I haven't pushed and pushed them. In fact, until '81 it was me saying 'You gotta take some time off to be with your families'. I'd seen how being on the road had destroyed things at home for other bands.

"The world tour was a matter of keeping interest growing for them. Argentina, India, Egypt, instead of the same thing over and over boring them to death. I have to interpret not just what the Police *say* they want, but what the Police *really* want." Management by telepathy?

When Miles talks of the Police he doesn't mean 'the band my brother's in'. Copeland blood can be earned as well as inherited. He muses: "We're not a dynasty in the

90

sense of being nepotistic. We include people like Sting, Andy and Kim Turner as members of the family even though they aren't. I mean Kim is a brother to me totally. Worked for nothing, saw problems and told me he'd fix them, never wanted anything. And now he's got 25 per cent of the management of the Police.

"We're all close. We fight each other and we fight for each other."

Stewart sums up why: "The Copeland brothers are an ethnic minority of three."

But he's worried. In mid-'81 Miles was planning to marry an American girl and Stewart was saying: "The people at A&M can't handle it. Just when they were getting used to slugging it out with him he's gone mellow on them. I always said as soon as he found eternal bliss he'd cease to be a great manager."

So it's a family affair. It has to be. The extraordinary demands of the band and the ordinary demands of home life have to be finely balanced or they would tear the group and families apart. That's why early in '81 wives/girlfriends/children began coming on the road with them, and part of the reason they opted for the long break immediately afterwards.

It affects them all in different ways. Even Andy, the original man in a suitcase, has felt the strain: "I've got a two-year-old daughter growing up and I'm going to miss the whole thing if I don't bring her on the road at least some of the time. It's become an emotional necessity because I want to see her and I want to see my wife."

In his candid way Stewart will talk about how the rock 'n' roll sex life relates to home and hearth: "The Police have gotten through a lot and that's why our family lives are about as tight as they can be. Sonja having been in bands helps me a lot. She comes to gigs now and sees these chicks working me over and she knows exactly what goes on but she doesn't let it bother her.

"I do have girls approaching me all the time and offering themselves. Not just slags and groupies you get hanging around, but married women too. At times it almost shocks me. I'll be sitting there talking politely with a famous record company executive and his wife when he wanders away and suddenly it comes out. It gets very weird.

"I don't find any urge at all to use my power over people in that way, honestly I don't. But also I have found out about myself that I'm a natural born flirt. And that can get me into trouble. So I don't flirt as much as I used to.

"The main point is that Sonja knows I'll be back whatever happens. I'm happy with what I've got and there isn't anything for her to worry about. When you add up what Sonja and I have been through together and the trust that we have I just don't think that I could find that anywhere else. I wouldn't have all those growth years in common with anyone else. They would be having a relationship with 'The Stewart Copeland', but with Sonja I know it's founded on the same me that I will be when all of 'The Stewart Copeland' is stripped away."

It's also of great importance to Stewart that he gets on very well with Sonja's son Sven, and he looked after him on his own on the last leg of the world tour. He recognized the stirrings of fatherly feeling in his heart and liked it a lot.

Sting is the most overt and passionate family man among the Police. In depressed moments he'll say "The only thing that's keeping me from drinking gallons of whisky or shooting up is my marriage. I know that without that firm solid love and trust and affection I would be a mental case."

He'll hold forth about Frances without reserve: "I needed someone who could cope with me, who isn't just an appendage to me. A partner. A *sparring* partner. Frances will fight back fiercely. I'm closer to her than anybody. She's my ideal I suppose. I'm very lucky. She's an intelligent, thinking, beautiful . . ." For once, words fail him.

Frances is a natural competitor too. When she takes a phone message about yet another movie offer for Sting she gets twinges of envy all right: "Partly I feel resentful, not so much for myself as for my whole profession that those opportunities should come to him so easily. All that attention he got from a small role in *Quadrophenia* when really good actors like Phil Daniels were ignored. But another part of me feels very happy that someone I love should be doing so well. Then again Sting is jealous of my successes too."

Although their careers have conveniently progressed in parallel and for the first year or more in London Frances was the main breadwinner, they certainly haven't achieved equality in caring for Joe, and Frances has sometimes felt bitter about that — especially as she found that she didn't like leaving him with child minders or in crèches.

This tension should be eased by the Police stepping off the treadmill, and for Sting, like Andy, the break will help him to get to know his child: "I'm a very serious father. Probably so serious I'll be dreadful at it. Oh God, I just wonder what Joe's going to make of it all. At the moment he's very good. Asked what his dad does for a living he said 'My father shouts and jumps up and down — but it's too loud for me'."

Their attitude to the groupie scene is opposite to Stewart and Sonja's. And the pressures on 'The Sting' are even greater.

Frances says fierily: "There's no such thing as 'open marriage' between us. We're both jealous as hell and utterly monogamous." Sting feels the same: "It's true. I'm very, very jealous too. I couldn't take that kind of . . . frivolity. I'm old-fashioned that way. The whole idea of 'Ah, it doesn't matter that much'. It does!"

Of course he gets asked a lot: "Oh yeah, I'm courted constantly. But . . . I never trust the reasons behind it. I do like beautiful women around and they are there. But *I do not give myself easily*. I won't jeopardize my position for a quick fuck. I also like remaining aloof. It's a perversion of mine really. Self-imposed isolation which I find very useful."

Sting certainly has no regrets that he was honest about his family from the first though some simple-minded pop moguls would say that a teeny idol has to be a potential husband to his girl fans and a footloose blade to the boys. Sting thinks that's all nonsense and a gross condescension: "Stewart wasn't sure about it at first, but it's a matter of 'I am what I am'. If anything it makes me more attractive. It's real sexuality, not like the Bay City Rollers — that's jerking off, kiss-me-quick. We're married men, we've had *it*. I think that's the point: with the Police you can actually get fucked."

9
OUTRO: HERE'S SHIRLEY, SHE'S A BIG FAN OF THE BAND

The Police are stinking rich. So what do they do?

Even they are daunted at times. "Great lumps of money," as Stewart calls them, sitting there in the bank. They won't just go away. Well, the Police wouldn't really want them to . . .

Sting, the former Marxist, still a socialist by his own lights, has moments when he just doesn't know where he stands: "I can't face the idea of being 'rich' even now. When I look at the accounts it's not mathematics, it's astronomy." Yet in a different mood he will say: "I've enjoyed every minute really. I find it very natural, very easy to assimilate what's happened."

If for Sting wealth is a mystery, a niggling thorn in the conscience, and a delight, there are no such ambiguities for Andy: "Money corrupting? To lesser mortals, yes (*his Puck smile*). In all honesty I don't think it makes the slightest difference to me. All it does is give you hopefully and eventually more time and facilities to try things. That's the only way I see it. I have no need for a Rolls Royce, but it is a joy that I can finally afford an eight-track Teac to record on at home. And I can play music without worrying whether it's going to sell or not. I've been trying for enough years; it's nice to reach that position."

One answer for those overburdened with cash is to give it away. The Police already do that on a large scale, though it makes only a minimal dent in their income, through their charitable foundation which receives all their earnings from gigs in the UK — even if it was set up essentially as an alternative to them paying most of the money to the government in tax anyway.

Sting's understandably confused political stance as a prosperous socialist emerges as he explains it. It seems to be cynical and good-hearted at the same time: "Maggie Thatcher is responsible for a saner attitude to megabuck earners. In the past Britain lost a lot of revenue because people like Rod Stewart thought 'Stuff this' and went off to America where they wouldn't be taxed so highly. The Tories created this loophole whereby if you spend nine months out of the country your foreign earnings are untaxed at home. That's the way out we've taken.

"I believe strongly that money is freedom and power. But to Thatcher, people without money can go to the wall. It's a deliberate economic measure, creating unemployment to keep inflation down. It's a disgrace, it's immoral. She's throwing a generation down the drain, she's completely wasting their talent and energy. That's one of the reasons I'm justified in not paying taxes. She's not building more schools, she's not feeding the kids who attend them, she's building sites for American nuclear warheads and sending working-class kids to get killed in Belfast. I'm not going to pay for it if I can help it.

"We made about £150,000 from our gigs in England in 1980 and that will all go to youth organizations largely to do with music, providing instruments and so on. It's professionally organized and it works."

Apart from that, Sting hasn't forgotten how to give personally. He and Frances send their £100 checks to the flood and earthquake funds as they arise. They also pay £150 a year to a scheme which supports the education of children in Kenya. For a couple of years they have been sponsoring a teenager called Achira.

The experience of wealth is still so new for Sting that perhaps it's more a matter of trying opinions on for size than being convinced. Self-awareness surfaces when he catches himself lounging against a dressing-room door with a bottle of Dom Perignon champagne in his hand and a crowd of 'liggers', themselves 'privileged' compared to the mass of actual fans, kept at bay by rope barriers and uniformed guards.

Even Miles, who is not known for making soulful remarks, suddenly blurts out the unease which gnaws at him when he's not concentrating on the process he promotes so frenetically: "I don't like going on the road except some place new. I hate just traveling. I *hate* it. I don't like living out of a suitcase, never having a social life, never having a personal life. Basically you have all this success and you're empty."

Stewart is eloquent about the way circumstances are constantly seducing him to lose touch with reality and become 'The Stewart Copeland': "I'm guilty of wielding the power of my position sometimes. Like going down Madison Square Garden to see Bruce Springsteen and lording it up. Snarling at people 'I don't need a fuckin' backstage pass'.

"But I get vertigo. My cup runneth over with adulation. I crack a joke, make a silly face and everyone falls about. I

Sting: "I decided that I could impose beauty on myself. As a result of a feeling . . . that it should be."

say something stupid, really uncool, I'm starting to cringe with embarrassment, I look up and they're still falling about.

"I went to an old friend's party recently and all the people there were Police fans and I could hear them whispering 'There's Stewart Copeland'. I'd be introduced to somebody and it was like 'Here's Shirley, she's a big fan of the band' and Shirley would go 'Ooo' and giggle and stuff. Most of the people I wind up going out with aren't really interested in the Police, probably don't have one of our records in their collection. They don't have to ask me questions about the tour or the album and I don't have to keep on saying 'Thank you'. I can feel that I have to compete and participate. I'm happiest when I've forgotten who I am."

For all his self-control Sting finds himself losing his grip of ordinary person-to-person communication too: "You have to force yourself to be interested in other people. Because you're so used to being the object of attention, just to have a normal conversation is very difficult. You feel yourself churning out your interview spiel."

So they can still step outside, they can still observe themselves. Their objectivity and self-knowledge haven't been wrecked by the first three years of madness. But there's always more. More flesh to press in the cause of promoting the band. Kim Turner admits to having no mercy when it comes to introducing people who might be of use to them at some stage: "All the hand-shaking has to be accepted. Say we're in New Orleans, I'll bring some guys down because we're not as big there as elsewhere in the States. No matter how much the band resent putting the hand out and saying 'Hallo, how are you doing?' to some DJ, two weeks later that guy will still be playing their record."

Sting grudgingly acknowledges Kim's argument. "There is still another ridge to climb — if we want," he says. If? One significant thing the Police were doing as they approached their much-needed break in spring '81

"I can't face the idea of being 'rich' even now." Sting (flanked by bodyguards).

was contemplating the possibility, however remote, of their end.

"I'm out for myself and Stewart and Andy know it!" says Sting. "As long as the group is useful for my career I'll stay. As soon as it isn't I'll drop it like a stone. The alternative is saying we're all in this for life. All for one, one for all. Fuck that. That's very limited. This is the longest job I've had. I want something else. It's not the whole 'Police Split!' thing, I'm not seriously suggesting that. But when we next play I'll have to really want it."

Stewart has heard Sting make similar speeches before and he rolls with the verbal punches: "The emotional level we work on means that it could explode at any moment and none of us would have any hold on each other. I could start wailing 'Oh no no no, Sting's going to leave the group!' But there's another element to it which is that Sting knows logically he'd be a fucking idiot to do it! What other situation is he ever going to be in like this? He's the star of the show. Everyone's running around for him. He is getting incredible amounts of money. Whereas in the movie world he'll have to work under directors and he can't say 'I'll be two hours late' or 'I'm canceling that' whenever he wants to.

"I think this is the best gig for him. But of course I do know that when it isn't off he'll go. He won't take that decision just because he's temporarily demoralized though. If he leaves the group it *will* be for a good reason, and if it's a good reason for him then it's a good enough reason for me."

So the Police will stay together – until they split up. But how do they stay alive as artists when in moments of black cynicism they can think as Sting has: "A million dollars from A&M on delivery of each album. Not an advance to be set against future royalties, but a part payment of *what they owe us* from past sales! And they have no control whatsoever over content , , , it's a great temptation to present them with an album of farting – and they'd be legally bound to give us the money.

"There's a part of me saying 'Fucking great! Rubbish next album!'. But if that was really the case I wouldn't want any more. I'd rather open a greengrocer's shop."

That's one of the cut-off points: when you start making records for the company rather than the public. At that stage the *only* product is money. So when they've bought all the synthesizers, Echoplexes, upright bases, movie cameras and houses they could possibly want, and girdled the globe into the bargain, where can they look for incentives?

They have to turn to aesthetics. This enticing and often misused word means 'the philosophy of the beauty of art'. Hardly an exact science, the science of 'soul' if you like, but important to the Police if you take their music as anything other than a means of selling baked beans on black vinyl platters.

When the going gets intellectual Stewart gets going. "This is great," he chortles. "Artists have to take themselves seriously. I mean when I'm writing a song I find it hard not to snigger at myself and here we are with the tape recorders going and the notebooks out. I love it.

"To a certain extent it's all bullshit. This is a theory I

formulated after 500 million interviews. One journalist comes up to us and says 'You recorded "Zenyatta" in three weeks. You shortchanged us because you're so busy making money you put out this piece of under-recorded half-baked product'. The next interviewer says 'How do you guys manage such an epoch-making album which revolutionizes music around the world and redefines the cosmos in only three weeks?'. It's the same record. It's just that one guy sees it one way and another guy sees it another."

That's aesthetics? No. He's just holding it up to the light and examining it from all sides. He asks: "Is art totally submersive and self-exploratory, or is it a method of communication? Because if it's communication, if it's 'speech' in some sense, then you can measure it in terms of how *many* people you speak to — maybe through a concert, or even in terms of record sales!

"But there's another dimension as well which is how *seriously* do you affect those people you speak to? Instead of measuring in volume you measure in intensity, how much you can actually get their hearts pounding, or get them crying ... without actually starting to worry them."

The Police surely have much more to pour out if they wish. They've set hearts pounding all right, but have they ever made anyone cry? They have been hot and exciting and they have reined back to a restrained melancholy which is their distinctive mood. But they have never really let go. And they could, Stewart is convinced: "Sting is basically a tragic character. Nearly all his songs are sad and his lyrics give the band that sort of personality."

That's where the Police's greatest potential lies and yet it's where they've been most inhibited. Their immaculate refinements have suppressed their 'soul' beyond a certain point.

Sting has already been beyond. With Last Exit at the Gosforth Hotel on a Wednesday night in 1976: beer mugs and conversation were clinking along until everyone realized the band had gone quiet and Sting was murmuring into the mike with a passion which in a second had the hair on the back of your neck standing on end. 'You and I are lovers ... I burn for you, I *burn* for you.' This sensuous glowing song with its slow crescendo remains the most moving performance Sting has achieved.

Early in 1981 he did two demos of the song and was obviously interested in exploring that unbridled emotion once more. It could unlock the Police's musical 'formula' and free their words from the precise logic of 'Don't Stand So Close To Me; or 'De Do Do Do'.

Perhaps there has been a glimpse of the band's more fruitful possibilities already in the 'Zenyatta Mondatta' track 'Shadows In the Rain'. On the album it has a haunted feel. It was a fragment of a song which Sting brought into the studio and the band embellished without ever taking the fine sandpaper to its rough surface.

Out on the road it became even more edgy. It was a risk in concert terms because it's lack of obvious movement weighed heavy on audiences and subdued them. It clearly wasn't 'commercial'. But it was 'intense' and it was 'seriously affecting the people it was speaking to' as Stewart says.

Andy Summers loves that song and it draws from him a stunning techno-poetic description of how he has responded to it with skill and emotion intertwined. Don't let the details worry you, just go with the flow: "The way we're playing it live now I think it's becoming a seminal number. A lot of people are being pulled up short by it. I found the guitar part after we'd recorded it. We started more or less from scratch in the studio. Sting had this old jazzy rhythm nothing like the version on 'Zenyatta' and we tried a lot of different things.

"I put on two guitar parts which complemented each other and made a weird reggae rhythm which we decided was an improvement, slower and more funky. Then I went in and laid the pseudo-psychedelic tape echo part all the way across, and everybody liked that. I did it by playing through an Echoplex with Stewart moving the tape speed up and down so it sounded like it was bubbling and twisting and turning the whole way. Obviously I couldn't do that live so I started working out this more orchestral part: chords with the echo and repeat wound all the way up so that when you hit the guitar the original sound *isn't* heard. All you hear is the echo, and I swell that up with the volume control, shhhhhhsht, and it's like a string section coming in.

"You've got to hit it just before the beat so that you don't hear the repeat of the echo, you just hear that great cloud of sound emerging. Combined with that I fragment all the chords. The chord structure is fairly basic, but I play them all in flattened fifths and invert them so that it sounds much more modern.

"I mean, the riff at the end when Sting sings 'Shadows in the rain' over and over is a basic A-minor, but I actually use a strange inversion of an A-minor sixth chord. It's high and as it starts to feedback I hit a high harmonic on the top string which echoes against the chord feedback and you start to get this whole new effect. You enter another world. I really like the dark, brooding quality of it. I think it's a good way for us to go."

You get the picture? Or do you feel flattened and inverted?

Meanwhile, back in New York, Sting was listening politely to a lot more critical gargling about aesthetics and the Police's need for expansion, extension ... "What you're saying is that there's vast room for improvement. It's true. My prime interest is the function of what we do. The function of my songs is that window cleaners sing them and people on factory floors sing them. Someone makes a vase and its purpose is to hold flowers. In retrospect someone might say 'Ah, Art!'. But in the early stages all you know is it's function."

He said again that "everything to do with the Police is frustrating at the moment, every aspect". He sat there for a while on the plush sofa in the 400-dollar-a-night hotel suite stewing about how things could be so good and so bad.

Then he surprised himself by stumbling on a cheering thought and looked up with a lighter face: "You know, one saving experience I've had in the last couple of weeks is going out on my own into the studio and coming up with a song which is incredibly happy, incredibly optimistic. I just can't wait to have more of that. In fact, have a listen to it..."

He handed over his Sony Stowaway and we listened to a demo of an exultant calypso. Perhaps you'll have heard it by now. It was called 'Everything You Do Is Magic'.

ALL COLOR PHOTOGRAPHS COURTESY OF LYNN GOLDSMITH.
COPYRIGHT 1981 LYNN GOLDSMITH INC.

BLACK AND WHITE PHOTOGRAPHS SUPPLIED BY:—

PAUL SLATTERY
RICK WALTON
C. SANDERSON
B.B.C.
PETER BAYLIS
L.F.I.
JUSTIN THOMAS
FIN COSTELLO
ALAN JOHNSON
GUS STEWART
B.F.I./ROAD MOVIES
WHO FILMS
AND LYNN GOLDSMITH